D1805779

Advanced LinkedIn

Attract the right opportunities with the use of LinkedIn by building an outstanding profile, creating content and regularly engaging with your connections.

FELIPE LODI

FIRST EDITION

© Copyright 2018 Felipe Lodi

All rights reserved. No part of this publication may be reproduced, stored in a retrieval system, or transmitted, in any form or any means (electronic, mechanical, photocopying, recording or otherwise) without prior written permission.

Advanced LinkedIn Logo created by Daniel Lodi.

Advanced LinkedIn - First Edition
Attract the right opportunities with the use of LinkedIn by building an outstanding profile, creating content and regularly engaging with your connections.

ISBN: 9781728744810

Contents

To my late Mother Suely who wrote Emails with the important text on the subject field. She already knew where brief communication was heading.

Foreword: Better Out Than In

Who would have thought that at the touch of a button we could contact almost anyone in the world? How can it be done you say? Through social media of course. The opportunities that social media present to us are in their infancy. As an author of several books, the host of a podcast show, and as a real estate professional, I use social media on a daily basis to build and promote my personal brand. My experience with social media has been hugely positive, so much so, that I would go as far to say that I would not have achieved some of my goals without this technology. It works like magic, I record a podcast, make a video, write an article, and boom! People all over the world can consume my material. This material is better out than in, as I can express who I truly am with these technology platforms. The messages and feedback I have received from people all over the world have been both heart-warming and humbling. It excites me even further to unlock what the future holds using social media. However, these opportunities are not just unique to me; you too can capitalise on them through the strategies you will learn in this book as the pages unfold.

I have the honour of knowing Felipe Lodi personally, and it really is a pleasure to call him my friend. Personal Branding and social media excites Felipe; it's one of his passions, he has dedicated a tremendous amount of time learning the key techniques and strategies on the topics. Now for the first time you too can learn the "secret" techniques Felipe has used to build such a successful personal brand and businesses. As a professional, Felipe's reputation precedes him, but as a person, Felipe is one of the kindest and most down to earth individuals that I know. Felipe always has his clients, and other people's interests at the forefront of his mind, so that he can bring them value or help them in some way. One of the things that I look for in an author is that if they practice what they preach, and it's easy to see that Felipe not only practices it, he lives it. You are learning from the master by reading this book, and it's an honour for me to have written the foreword to such a great book.

Social media and personal branding can often be overlooked. However, Felipe has simply laid it out so that you can take advantage of their opportunities. For example, having a strong personal brand can lead to getting more job interviews in your dream career field or if you are a public speaker it can help you grow your audience. The possibilities are endless and now you in your hand you're equipped with the best tool in the business. So, make the most of this book, let your mind be blown, push outside your comfort zone, but most importantly implement your learning. As I said, it's better out than in!

Gerard Bissett
Author and Podcast Host

LinkedIn as a Sales Platform

This book is a documentation of what I've achieved so far with the use of LinkedIn and how I attracted job opportunities, clients for my businesses and unthinkable partnerships. In two years, I went from a successful Software Developer and Consultant to a people-person and a reference to a micro-niche of professionals. My online exposure brings me so many businesses and opportunities that I decided to give it back by writing this book.

I decided to put this together this for two reasons: I needed to show people evidence that no one gets to their dream job or succeed in business without networking (and that your network is not made by your first level connections only as I will show you in the book.) And the second reason is that I cannot stress enough how LinkedIn is the perfect fit for that.

I held over fifty gatherings such as workshops and small conferences in the Republic of Ireland in 2017 and 2018 about Personal Branding and Advanced LinkedIn. The subjects were not unexplored in the country but it looked to my team and me that no one was holding free events like we were doing: what was justifiable considering that we were new to the arena of coaching and personal development by then and the free admittance was an excellent way to make people aware of us.

This gave us experience with the subjects as it helped us understand what professionals were demanding and how naive they were regarding not being exploring Social Media as much. That also created and improved our content, shortened our pitch and gave us exposure to the public and private sectors in the country. Such content that is also being repurposed into this book now.

Yes, we have competition, I have competition as an Influencer. I don't give them another thought, though, but the evidence that I have is that no one around has an established and proven methodology about LinkedIn, and a direct approach that can help Jobseekers, Students, Moms, Entrepreneurs, Immigrants, Human Resources representatives, Recruiters, Coaches and Trainers explore LinkedIn and benefit from what I call "let the tool work for you." mindset.

If you decide to read this thing by now, you will see that LinkedIn is an interesting tweakable tool. And I don't mean that you can go to the settings screen and customise the notifications, etc. I mean that defining the type of content that you will be putting on and establishing yourself as a leader in a specific industry was never so easy to achieve in the history of professional and personal relationships. In a matter of two weeks, following what I propose here, you will get the first results (and sometimes even sooner.)

If you permit me making the analogy here, creating and posting content about your industry on LinkedIn is like having a tent selling water on a desert. You will have a limited public, but everyone will know that they must come to you to the items that only you have. Therefore, LinkedIn is pretty much like this; you can claim your spot on a specific niche, in a particular region and become the "go to" reference.

I could probably become a reference in another subject matter in a few weeks if I applied what I will show you with the book. That would perhaps create some controversy with my public, but LinkedIn is so powerful that the tool itself would help me explaining why I changed from Learning and Development to Neuroscience. A couple of a few posts and articles and raw pictures of me attending to congresses and I have a new network of scientists (Nope, I am not changing, just making a point here.)

What is also spectacular with LinkedIn is that you don't need to have tens of thousands of connections to improve people's lives and yours like you would need on Instagram, Facebook or Twitter. With a couple of a hundred connections, you are good to go! If you go and check the number of connections that I have at the time that I am writing this book, you might be frustrated (a little bit over 3800.) But don't judge my online exposure by that. Judge by the stories that I will tell you throughout this book and make a projection that if I have all this happening to me with such a small number of connections, imagine if I had ten times more. Imagine if you had ten times more after practising the learnings in this book.

And I have a good number of haters too! Yes, they are so necessary. I like them as much as like the people who follow me. As I monitor the gap between the number of connections that I have on LinkedIn and the number of followers, I see that a proportion of ten per cent stopped following me through the years, and I know exactly why this happens, but I will leave this to another topic later in the book.

This book is about the relationship and how this is paramount for attracting good things for you. Relationships that you will create with the use of LinkedIn (e-relationships, or perhaps, in relationships as I just thought of coining.) In the end, if everything we do in life is for increasing the number of relationships we have, and improving the quality of the relationships we have, so why not use relationship building for that?

This book will show you how to make yourself visible by documenting and displaying every step you take towards a goal and getting respected as you go and not only after you get there. LinkedIn enables and boosts your possibilities with an extreme likelihood of success. And I am here to help you avoid the procrastination and the fact that professionals who are still in their social constraints are missing the point here. The time that you needed to leave your achievements talk by themselves is gone. Now you have to achieve and display. Accomplish and document. Benefit and brag. People will criticise you, and that will be the best sign that things are working out for you online. Be ready for that.

Well, I trust that I convinced you to keep reading the book by now. LinkedIn helped me write this piece not because it is a favourite theme but because the daily use of the tool made me leave my anti-social bubble when I realised that I would never make everyone happy. This book will bring me a lot of criticism, but it will bring much more concerning recognition and relationship. When I created the habit of writing publicly on the tool about what I think, what I do and the way I do it, and these brought me businesses and friends, I thought, why not going the extra mile and leaving a legacy in the shape of a book.

People Don't Care About What You Think

People don't care about what you think unless you're talking directly to them. And with Social Media is no different. You need to be using appealing content to attract the people who will identify with what you are sharing as well as with the way you think. You need to practice the same technique the Filmmakers do when they bring components to movies that make people relate and leave the theatre talking about the movie they watched to others.

With Social Media, the difference is that by

ON LINKEDIN, YOU DON'T NEED TO HAVE TENS OF THOUSANDS OF CONNECTIONS.

attracting the people who like the same subjects as you, you are creating your network and your followership. Are they going to buy from you or hire you? Not necessarily. But they will advocate for what you think and on which Like or Share they make on the content you produce, you are potentially amplifying the reach of your content as well as the awareness upon your profile. That is what you want to achieve.

And that is why I mentioned earlier that having a small number of connections does not matter much. Again, what is important is the quality of these connections. Being connected with the people who will relate to your content is what matters the most. Do not ever forget that.

Therefore if you are in business or looking for a new job in your industry, you will need to increase the connections with the people who will either buy from you or with the people who will be in the companies where you want to work. That is one of the most significant differences between Facebook and LinkedIn. Regardless of the fact that most people will use Facebook as an actual Social Network, or the useless friends and family network, Facebook's algorithms will not put you together with people in your industry unless you go there and tell them that you want to join the group about the specific theme you want to be involved. To be more precise, Facebook recently implemented changes that removed institutional Shares and unpaid advertisements from the feeds of people connected with you. I felt a substantial drop in the number of views and reach upon these types of posts that I always did.

Luckily this book is not about Facebook, though I also believe that the tool is extraordinary. LinkedIn, on the other hand, will keep related content in a better way, but you will need to do the legwork. You will need to research, read, learn, curate and nurture your followers (or the people connected with you) for this to start creating opportunities for you. More on that to come.

Let's get back a bit now and think about when you meet a person for the first time outside Social Network. You are at the Gym, waiting for your kid to leave the Ballet class or by the pool in a fancy holiday break at the Bahamas. If you start chatting with an unknown person and for some reason, the talk progresses to work-related stuff, and they ask: "How about you? What do you do?" In the next five seconds of interaction, you have a short but rich moment to pitch whatever you like, to play whatever role you want to play. We will be developing the "Pitch" subject further in the book, but my point here is that you can make whatever impression you like because of two things: The person does not have a pre-concept about you, and the person is paying attention to you for at least five seconds.

With Social Media is the same. You will need to build an impression that will fit into the way people behave nowadays. The so-called "short spans of attention." Especially the way people flick their fingers down on their phones. You will want to print into people's brains the connection between your industry, your name, picture and tagline (more on the Tagline and picture further in the book.) Even though with the Social Media you have less than the five seconds as in an actual conversation to grab attention, your content will be creating this "magic" about your profile several times a day, to as many people as it can reach, and while you sleep (or are in an actual conversation in a beach in the Bahamas.)

So, in theory, you can project your image as a Jet Pilot, Racecar Pilot, or Spaceship Pilot. The Social Media, and specially LinkedIn, is so powerful that if you start posting, sharing and creating content about any of these professions, you will quickly raise questions from the people will already know, making unknown people believe that you are a pilot and I don't doubt that opportunities will also appear for you in this arena.

You have a rich environment, therefore, if you plan to nurture your followership with content related to your real life, and your real profession, the chances are on your side. You are going to get it if you apply yourself to it.

LinkedIn is a Professional and a Social Tool

Is LinkedIn a Professional or a Social Tool? You won't find the answer for that anywhere. So you will have to take a stand now. You will find opinions from people who are trying to make your content better for their eyes. Let them unfollow you when you post that nice picture of your meal with the copywriting saying that you are celebrating passing on an interview. Be used to be judged and be indifferent to that. We live in times when we decide what to watch on Netflix, we decide whom to follow on YouTube, and we decide no longer signing for cable TV and paying to watch advertisements. I decided that. At home, we only signed up for the broadband, and you should do that too. There is no way back (thank God), and you must think of your LinkedIn profile as your TV channel about your life. You will have an editorial calendar that I will teach you how to do it. You will have scheduled posts and measure their results. You will learn how to make split tests and narrow down your audience until you get only the people who will like how you balance the level of professional and social posts. I know, you weren't expecting this, and you are now deep down in the book you bought it. You only wanted to make a few adjustments on your profile, and I am now asking you to become a content producer on LinkedIn. Well, no pain, no gain. Without making yourself visible in the network, I am afraid to say, your opportunities won't come, and you will be left alone with your endless job applications or cold calling (if you are in Sales), trying to be respected by bagging together with the majority of people. Take a stand now; it is time to decide which type of professional you want to be. A professional who has a voice, a professional who has the power of creating opinions, even if those opinions are that they don't like the type of posts you are doing. They are still opinions that you are forming. If they don't like your opinion, they won't buy or hire you anyway, but on the other hand, when they like what you say, they will throw opportunities at you. And that is what I will make happen to you. The content, whether professional or social, is the vehicle for your success. You will reach notoriety, and you will stay there as long as you want.

At the end of 2015, my wife and partner in all my businesses decided to change the business model of our main company. From an IT Contractor, we expanded to Human Resources with the mission to help mitigate the lack of talent in the Republic of Ireland. The only people who knew us were our close network of friends, a few employees and clerical workers of the companies that we used to have as clients (still in the IT arena.) I was in a rant reading three to four books a month about starting-up, Social Media, management and leadership. They all referenced the creation of content as key for succeeding in any venture. I realised that content can come in multiple forms and that as a Leader, I would need to create it and find the best format that would resonate with an audience that we didn't have yet. We took the route of holding free workshops for small groups of people. The audience would come to a room with a capacity of eight people, and I vividly remember struggling to fill the room. Even though the events were free, people didn't know us; they didn't know me. We invest from our own pockets to give them gifts and making the best atmosphere, but that wasn't what they wanted. They wanted to learn new things. So I noticed that the more I would bring new subjects and debate new ideas, the more they would come back. I didn't know by them, but we were building our sales pipeline. We were generating new content, I was improving my presentation skills, and people were starting to see us as a reference for a determined set of subjects. We held twenty-eight free events between the end of 2015 and 2017 and sales took off. That was starting to pay off. I will tell you way more about, and how the network created with such initiatives led us to new business ventures and recognition in the market. For instance, we I write this book, we launched a new free event about LinkedIn with a big Bank in Ireland, and 180 tickets vanished in three days. A personal best if compared with how we struggled to fill a room with eight people.

And I will always keep recommending people to be social on professional networks. I will still suggest that you should be entertaining people so that they stick with you. And don't ever underestimate the challenge of being interesting. Being entertaining and interesting is not the same as being funny, remember that. I haven't cracked that down yet completely; I am still trying things to understand what plays well and what doesn't. I found the right balance between social and professional posts, though, and how to place useful advice in a post that catches the eye of people because they thought they would have been entertained on their Monday morning. Too late, they have been advised to grow, and they felt that they would have been tickled.

The truth is that LinkedIn tries every day to become more of a social tool, and Facebook tries every day to become more of a professional tool. I see those posts saying "let's keep LinkedIn professional," or "let's not allow LinkedIn to become Facebook." Wrong, so wrong in believing that there has to be a separation whereas we all should be thinking that the type and characteristics of your content should be the same, regardless of the network. The Media you will use in one network or another will change, the frequency and the length too, but the essence of the message that you want to pass will not. Regardless of the network.

You must work to leverage a professional network on Facebook where the groups and communities are way more powerful than on LinkedIn. You must work to leverage friends and family on LinkedIn where the ripple effect of a Like or Share on connections' timelines is way more effective than on Facebook. I lecture on classrooms, and I am constantly surprised by the fact that the thirty people in the audience have been together for a month and they are not connected on LinkedIn yet. What?! That sends me a clear message that people believe that they should be connected to Recruiters only for their opportunities to appear. Silly them. Believing that they should put their hopes in a group of people who believe they are commodities whereas they should be investing in connecting to every single person they are related in their everyday's lives.

You are wrong, and you have been using LinkedIn in a very limited way. The same way you are not using the power of Facebook. You are not joining groups on any place and not exposing your skill set to people in your industry. You are in Chemistry, and you are not filming those nice experiments you do at the University's Laboratory. You are in Sales, and you are not bragging about how many new leads you convert. You are in Digital Marketing, and you are not posting anything online. You are a Programmer, and you are not writing Phyton manuals not for the sake of the readers but for the sake of creating social trust. Nobody knows you. You have this untriggered and encapsulated wisdom, but you are not a reference, yet. Let's remedy that.

In this book, I will show you how you will

LINKEDIN TRIES
EVERY DAY
TO BECOME A
SOCIAL TOOL,
AND FACEBOOK
TRIES EVERY DAY
TO BECOME A
PROFESSIONAL
TOOL.

connect automation tools to the three major networks where you will start posting content related to your industry. We will also discuss the types and format of the content you will be posting and how often you will be doing it. We will be posting social things to LinkedIn and professional stuff to Facebook. You will be criticised, and that will be the best sign that you are shaking worlds. People will stop following you at a different rate than people will start following you. You will notice a shift on the connections you once had, and this will be awesome for you because this will keep you closer to that network that can benefit you. Do not ever underestimate the opportunities that can come to you because of your new and amplified reach. You will be reaching out to people on all continents who relate to your subject matter. You will see how rewarding it is having someone in the United States or Australia linking and sharing your stuff that they believed would resonate with their audience. Will they buy or hire you? Not likely. Will the people closer to you buy or hire you? Likely to happen now as they notice how you have been talking with people from abroad. They will judge that you are "important." Social networks are displays of ignorance and wisdom, that is how the game is played now. You post a picture with a deskmate; your Views increase, your post a picture with the keynote speaker, your Likes increase, you post a picture with a celebrity, your sales increase. Noticed something here? These are social posts. Should you be restrained to use Facebook or Instagram to these or should you use LinkedIn where the majority of your professional connections will be to play this card?

It will take you a little while for you to equalise the number and quality of connections you have on all the networks. I am still a bit behind on Facebook, and I must admit, I just started in the Instagram game. I regret, and I don't want you to make the same mistake. Be aware and everywhere. Be frequent and consistent. Let's help you become that Epidemy we spoke about it. Let's annoy people until they send you a private message complaining about the frequency of posts you do (it happens to me.) Let's meet acquaintances on the streets and hear them saying "Wow! You have been so active on LinkedIn lately!" You will notice that you haven't seen that person liking or sharing anything you posted, and you will realise that your reach is actually broader than you thought, and that your pipeline is actually longer than you previously believed, and that things will only get better for you from now on.

The Path to Work
Using LinkedIn

Using the LinkedIn as your tool of choice for your professional growth will require strategy and perseverance. This book will show you how I did it, but I advise you to use it as a reference to your version of my method. For the simple fact that if you find what suits you best you will have better chances to keep up with it, and as it will require your daily work, it will also need to be pleasant. There are many small routines and practices that we will be discussing throughout the book, and they all fit into the three significant steps I am describing now. Adapt your activity on LinkedIn to your time but don't leave any of the three topics in this chapter out of your routine. Dedicate time for it. Spend less time on Instagram and Facebook and shift your efforts to LinkedIn for the time being. Use the tools that I will recommend in the final chapter of this book. Invest in having your artwork done too. I will explain in-depth what I mean by that.

Moreover, invest time in participating in conversations and engaging with people. People will bring the opportunities to you not LinkedIn. LinkedIn is programmed to enable your success and facilitate your work. I won't detail it here, but LinkedIn has evolved significantly since it had launched more than one decade ago. Come with it. Be the first to use the first feature, the first to click on that option, the first to explore a new field they make it available. It is a business for them, but it is for you in the first place.

Profile Optimisation.

Let's start by setting something in stone here. Goals are not dreams. The Dream word is a beautiful word, but to me, it addresses something that almost never can be achieved. So let's give special attention to the terminology we use as this will help you keep focused. The Goal word, on the other hand, is stronger and addresses to the finish line, something that will require your celebration and that can be broken down to smaller steps, feasible for everyone to achieve.

And that is what we are doing here, the three steps in this chapter will split the methodology, and they will give you a North towards your primary goal with the use of LinkedIn, which is using your network and the network of your connections to attract opportunities for you.

You won't get too far if you don't invest time in rebuilding your profile. I say rebuild because I know that there is no way that you already have your LinkedIn page built in the way that I will recommend here, with all the alternative components that I idealised. Therefore, you will need to concentrate a lot of the work now at the beginning so not only will that give you the confidence to progress through the method, but it will also separate you from the people who will not win with the use of the tool. Therefore the profile comes; first, it will be cumbersome for you to do it, but if you do it, I can tell you, you will have real chances to keep up with the work considering that the other two steps that I break this methodology into are less harder to maintain.

Your new profile needs a format. A format that will lead the viewer to understand your goals and why your professional background led you to pursue these goals. Your new profile will be more consistent with the image you want to project rather than the one that is not working the way you want. It is about telling the world what you want so you can get it. Not that simple, of course, but the perception people have upon your persona.

I have a lot of Students coming to us buying our preparation and asking how they can project their expertise if they don't have proven professional experience yet. See what I did here? I put the word "Proven" to trick you, and I ask: Who is to say that your experience needs to be proven? The Recruiters? You want to avoid words that will put roadblocks in front of your goals. You might not have experienced paid work in a corporation yet, but I am sure that you did a lot of work to get your nice and shiny diploma. I beg you to start believing that if you were finishing college or another graduation, you will start telling people that you have proven work in a laboratory, in a library or the computer camp. These are valuable resources for the market, and you would not believe how companies are craving fresh and new talent, especially the Millenials.

Recreating your profile will require creativity and some boldness to refactor to the current time all the work you have done. Paid or unpaid, proven or unaccounted, it will be up to you to project that successful image that will make people believe that you are the right fit.

Another crucial recommendation is that you work in your new profile at once. You are now reading this book and thinking about when and how you will create your new "You" online. Probably thinking about all the things you need to do in addition to this new task that I am giving you. But I want you to think about setting up a few hours for what is essential for you to or else the consistency you need to bring to your message won't be strong enough on your profile. If you do that in multiple days, you will find that reviewing what you wrote up to that point will bring second thoughts and you won't get anywhere trying to get to perfection. For instance, I wrote this book in ten days during my holidays at the Canary Islands. I knew that I wanted to set time for it and that if I stayed in my base office in Dublin dealing with Emails, meeting clients and helping with the deliveries, I would not do it due to the scattered work with the book. During the time that I blocked to have with the family, I could not be spending with anything but with their interests. What I did? I woke up every day at 5 AM, and I wrote for four hours every single day without jeopardising my time with them. It is always about figuring out how to deliver what is important to you.

You must dedicate a Sunday afternoon apart, and finish the thing. Put all the distractions away. Turn off your phone (reviewing your LinkedIn profile in your mobile is part of the process, but you will do it later) and turn Email reminders off, computer sounds and everything that can distract you from achieving your goal. Your new profile on LinkedIn will require images and artwork as well as gathering your personal files. The words are more important now, though. So if you must break the work, you first collect the artwork and documents needed for your profile (more on that to come) and then you type your stuff. Don't multitask between finding your files and writing. It won't work.

You would be surprised how people can make up time for their Tinder profile and Facebook page when it suits them. If attracting opportunities while you sleep is important for you, you will follow up with the learnings herein. I trust you will. The optimisation of your profile will give you the confidence to reach out to people, and when you do it, they will believe you for the mere fact that you are showing an organisation with your profile. It indicates subliminally that you want to go beyond where you are now.

I also want you to think about your profile as your "breathing CV." For those who are not into finding a new job opportunity, please allow me to call your professional background as CV for the sake of an efficient terminology here. I understand that for

I ALSO WANT YOU TO THINK ABOUT YOUR LINKEDIN PROFILE AS YOUR BREATHING CV.

Entrepreneurs, thinking about having a CV might look like a step back, but not in this case as you will need to describe the very same components of a person who is looking for a job opportunity.

So, your breathing CV is the actual paper CV you have (as I usually call, the boring CV) that will now become this living being capable of doing things on your behalf. You will nurture and feed it until it blooms and brings you concrete results, so I want you to think that every term that you type down on your new profile has a role to play. If you must repeat a word, you will research synonyms to that word so that you can amplify the reach of your keywords. You will also sound like a person who has a rich vocabulary, and you will still bring the meaning that you want to your sentence or paragraph. You will use a tool called Grammarly (they don't sponsor me, yet) to type in their pad every text before it goes to your LinkedIn profile. It will fix your commas, correct your grammar, and offer you the Isynonms. Signup for their three months subscription or use it for free with limitations, but please invest time in finding proper and industry-related vocabulary. Every detail counts.

There are three main sections on your LinkedIn profile that will require your creativity: The Summary, the Tagline and the descriptions of your career path. Yes! You noticed. LinkedIn does not use these terms in their field labels, but we will associate them with our new words here. It is about our modern terminology, remember? The Summary is that big block of text where you can describe yourself. I am not telling you here how many characters you can put in it so that I can keep this book current with multiple versions of LinkedIn, but you can tell a lot about your story there. Then you have the Tagline component that the majority of people will either let LinkedIn customise with the current job position you have or as many LinkedIn losers do, they put things like "Open to Opportunities" or "LION Networker" (a lot more about the "dont's" on LinkedIn to read in this book.) And finally, the descriptors of your career path, where for each job you had in the past, each company, each client, with the dates and references to their company pages, you will write about what that was all about. You will break each descriptor in two smaller sections called "Responsibilities" and "Key Achievements". Under each header, you will list using bullet points what were your responsibilities in that company or with that client or project and what was achieved there (LinkedIn won't give you the headers or formatting options to create the bullet points so you will need to be creative there.)

I will be describing all these components in depth during the next chapters, so don't put the book away now and start building your profile. I know that you are excited but trust me, you will have a lot to digest before you can work on your new profile. And if by now you realised that you will need to put a lot of work in it, you are right, you will. And that is the second time we separate the winners from the losers. The first was when you got this book.

Content Authoring

I love this part because most people give up. During the workshops and classes we do, I usually scan the room and stare at a few people of the audience when I tell them that they will need to create content on LinkedIn every day, several times a day. It is a mix of encouraged but doubtful faces and sceptical attitudes when I tell them that the content is the vehicle for the opportunities and without it, I cannot stress that enough, there is no way you will set yourself as a leader in your field.

As I go explaining that content creation is broken down from small thoughts written in a LinkedIn post to finished articles with images and references the credible faces improve, and I can move on with my seminar. And when I said that most people will give up at this stage not only do I want to challenge you to get to your goals, but I also want to show you that when people don't succeed on something is their fault. They didn't do the needful despite all the information they have access. It would be a shame because with the pieces of evidence that I will describe in this book, following up with the required is like baking a cake. You will partly stick to the recipe and slightly tweak to your own needs and routines. The bottom line is that without the content your profile will be a static one, and it won't play to your benefit. You will need to keep applying for jobs or chasing new clients every day. How has that been working for you so far?

What is also great about the content that you will be posting on LinkedIn is that you won't create that for people to read. They won't, in fact, perhaps not even your own authored pieces. What you want in reality is to create an association between your face, your Tagline and the type of content that you are posting. You also want to show them that you are a person of opinion. Well, everyone is, but very few can break the "I am too scared of what people think about me" barrier. Think like if you were narrowing down people through your sales funnel. You will post online, and some of your connections will drop. You will keep posting, and the remaining connections will think "Jeez, there's this thing now that she keeps doing...annoying." Then, some unfollow you. You will keep posting, and you will see the number of views increase as the gap between the connections and followers also increase (more on that too.) You will keep posting, and you will see the first Likes and Shares, great! You will keep posting, and someone drops you a private message asking if you know that guy Bob who is also in the same industry as you. (Yeap! It is working now. You are in a conversation.) You will keep posting, and a new client or a person from inside a company drops you a private message asking if you would be available for a coffee. (It worked now. You are becoming a reference.) When that happens, you will be close to a new job or a new client.

Of course, there is much more to it. It won't work perfectly like this, and there are nuances to it. You will put the work and wait a little while to see the first results. You will be ignored at first. It is like if the people connected with you were not expecting this from you. They will criticise you too (inside their heads, don't worry) and then they will take a decision to either praise you, keep following you, ignore you or remove you entirely from their timelines. All of sudden you will become a content creator, with another level of exposure, with your followership and daily conversations with people in your industry.

If you bear with me now let me tell you that this "Natural Selection" is the best thing that can happen to your professional profile. You want to know who is with you. Who empathises with your content and with your persona. And there is no other way to survey your audience without pushing content at them. I called content the vehicle because it sounds better than a driller, but this is actually what you are doing, you are drilling down and filtering who can potentially drive opportunities for you. And the beauty is that LinkedIn will do that for you if you work the way they expect you to do it if you build the ideal profile to their environment.

You might be asking whether you should interact with the people reacting to your content. Yes, you must. And that is the third step of our method that will boost your exposure. You can opt out the engagement, but it will look to people as if you were a celebrity. Not yet, right? You want to be accessible, and you want to be congenial. You want to be personal when approaching people and you want to be collaborative. You want to give first before you can receive. You want to show who you are going to be when they give you the job or the sale. You want to use every little opportunity to sell yourself without actually selling. It is a display, and I am not ashamed to write about it.

Constant Engagement

There are multiple levels of engagement. A Like on someone else's post is an engagement. So is a Share and a Comment. Sharing an article you just read and automating the Shares of the content you read is also engagement. You are signalling that you read, that you read regularly and also telling people that you do that very often. Your audience will be impressed and stop scrolling when they see your face in their timelines. Remember, you are already in the process of posting, narrowing down your followership for a few weeks now. Therefore the people who are arguably stopping to see what you posted were already tested against the

I WANT TO CHALLENGE YOU TO GET TO YOUR GOALS BECAUSE WHEN PEOPLE DON'T SUCCEED IS THEIR FAULT.

new virus "You."

That is pretty much what you want to be: A Virus. We won't discuss here Facebook, Twitter, Pinterest, Instagram, Google Plus, apart from a few mentionings, but you want to be anywhere all the time. Like an epidemy. People will remember your industry and remember about you. It works like that. But you will need to engage precisely the way I will suggest you do it. There will be tools to help you, don't worry. Yes! We all use automation tools. They are designed to help us. Most of them will not charge you anything until you become a Pro. When you become a Pro, you will feel like paying them to do more for you, and it will be worth it.

Automation tools will help you gather and organise and post content on your behalf. While you sleep. But you will need to do most of the legwork in finding the right content, coordinating and scheduling the content so that it is posted in the ideal times. Tracking the results of your engagement to see what times the majority of your audience is online. On LinkedIn, there are specific times such as Sunday evening that you should not be anywhere close it. Well, that is why I proposed you to work on your stuff on a Sunday. Unless you live or work with clients in the Middle East, Sundays will also be perfect for you to consuming content, learning and selecting what to schedule. We will be discussing content creation deep down in the book. I am still convincing you here.

And there is plenty of engagement that is manual. Do you know that little thing called Mobile Phone? That is your best partner now. Drag and drop the icon of your LinkedIn App to the shortest distance to your pointer finger. Do you know the people who tell you that you should not spend much time on it? This book and my methodology are not for them. You want to double, triple, quadruple down the use of your device. With the advantage now that you will have people engaging back to you in a way that the first thing you will do when you wake up in the morning is to check the notifications on your phone to see how your social currency is performing.

Be vain, be bold and be connected all the time. We will be discussing posting personal things and the cute photo of your Burger to LinkedIn as well. Surprised? Haters will love the picture of your Guinness (I live in Ireland.) And you don't want to limit yourself to industry-related posts only when you are putting off over fifty professional posts a week. You will show them that you have a life, took holidays, started cycling to work and went for a coffee with a client. There are plenty of opportunities in the texts you put together with the photo of a Convention Center you are getting inside.

Recently we had a corporate client of ours posting the celebration of the one year anniversary of their company. They took a photo of them popping a bottle of Champagne, and the text mentioned my name and the name of my partner as the enablers of their success. None of that. Though we appreciated the praise, and we know that they are grateful, what they wanted was to tell to their audience, (and to our viewers, since they tagged us) that their Investment Boutique was turning one. They continuously post professional content about Startups and financial matters. Therefore their "Social" content didn't hurt anyone but improved their reputation as successful people. And their prospects are now a step closer to buy from them, and so are ours.

See what I just did? I used this little story to show you an example. I advertised the fact that we work with corporate clients and help their Social Media thrive by using a real story. I could have said "Client", but I said "Corporate Client." I tried to sell you our product, and you didn't feel offended. I paid their bet and raised another stake. That is one of the examples of the leverage that you want to bring to your content.

The LinkedIn Profile Structure

We learned about the threefold strategy that will make you attract opportunities on LinkedIn. You probably figured out by now the amount of work that you will need to put on it. I will remind you again that it is going to be worth it. I have so many opportunities coming to my lap every week, and I am fortunate to have assembled a team of high performers that help me go for almost anything that shows. Even my team was assembled because of my exposure using the tool. As an Entrepreneur, one of the most important things that I learned is that is can be as hard as making a sale, convincing someone to work with you. But it is as equally as incredible to see how people throw themselves at you when they believe in your mission. The very mission I have been gravitating my content around during these past exciting years.

My profile changed and it is still evolving from the figure of a geek software developer who worked for brands such as IBM, Dell and the European Commission to the figure of the successful Entrepreneur that I am. Am I successful? Well, if success for you means owning a boat and a Chalet in Switzerland, I am still far away from it. But if success for you is the constant accomplishment of your goals, you got it, and you will check on my LinkedIn profile how I publicly document every step of my endeavours.

People also ask me very often whether they should reflect their transitioning career on LinkedIn, and I say "Hell Yeah! You must." Some will admire you, and some will despise you. As everything else in life and as you will on your new LinkedIn.

So, let's get to it. Let's start rebuilding your profile in this chapter. You won't see any pictures or screenshots in this book. I didn't want to have this resembling another boring manual. I trust, however, that my dedicated words will be plenty for you to understand what I need you to do it. Let's read first and do the work on that Sunday evening as I suggested. I am the biggest advocate of multitasking but let's not, for now.

Your Profile Url

Did you know that you can change how the unique Url of your profile look? That is an easy one, and you want to do it fast so that you can grab the best suitable address for your new profile. I know that you will tell me now that you don't use Twitter or Pinterest as much, and that is fine, but do you have accounts in these networks? Facebook you have, right? What is the Url of your Facebook profile? Can you change it too? Because I want you to have the same Url on all the networks. Well, not the full Url, of course, but the final part of the address, usually the part that can be customised.

It might be easier for you to grab your unique name on LinkedIn than on Facebook or Instagram, so let's check these two first. Can you use your first and last name combined? Is it already taken by someone else? Great! I am a positive person, and I know that you will be able to grab your unique name but if you can't, let's throw your middle name in it. Avoid things like including your profession in your Url because you can change your profession in the future. That is like having a matchmaking Tatoo.

As you push content on LinkedIn (as we will see in detail later in the book) you will feel the urge to start pushing content on all networks to amplify your reach. This book is not about Social Media, but you must think about your overall strategy having LinkedIn in the middle, and having the same alias (or term at the end of your Url's) will tell the Search Engines that you are the same person connected to a massive amount of content in your industry. You want to think long term here, and since I know that you will feel like posting professional things to other networks as well, you don't want to be identified as a different person on each network.

Got it? Let me go more in-depth here. I use the hook (or Alias) "felipelodi" on all networks. Well, I grabbed the term a while ago, and the only network that I couldn't claim my name was Snapchat (which I don't use, yet.) Though my surname "Lodi" is not common, I would have been challenged a few times during these years since I have seen a few felipelodi1, and felipelodi2 and so. What if I was pushing content on LinkedIn as felipelodi and on Instagram as felipelodi10. Would the Search Engines be identifying me as the same person? I don't think so. Every effort would have been split into two different streams. Not ideal, right? On the other hand, because I use the same name on all, the Internet organism thinks of me as the professional involved with Learning and Development, Personal Branding, EDTech, HRTech and Startups. And that is crucial to create credibility upon my persona and attract opportunities to me and my businesses.

Trust me. You want to do this exercise now. When you see the automation tools later in this book and realise that you can effortlessly schedule content on multiple networks, you will want to be the same person everywhere. Part of the epidemy you will cause.

Your Header Image

LinkedIn allows you to modify the header background of your profile. If you haven't touched your profile lately, the chances are that you have the dull blue image LinkedIn puts by default. Let's find a royalty-free image on the Internet that resembles with what you do as a professional. Just by changing that background image your profile will already look more engaging. Go to a Website called "Unsplash" as they have great photographers making their amazing pictures available for free. You will surely find something related to your industry to use as your background image.

Better than the industry-related image are the pictures taken from you on stage, on a meeting, at your desk, shaking hands with Gary Vaynerchuk or your Selfie with the Pope. People will relate better and trust you immediately when you display any success. As you may know, our brains interpret images way faster than words. In a time and age when our attention span shortens, you want to create rapport on the tenth of a second when people hit your profile to see who is the new guy in town posting all this content to their timelines.

And you can also produce your artwork to use as the background image of your profile. Our LinkedIn product, for instance, gives the subscribers a custom-made image using their professionally taken photo assembled with either their problem-solving Tagline or a chart depicting their skills. It is also an excellent way to send a message to the visitors of your profile that you came to claim your spot. And that is what you are doing now reading this book. I appreciate that.

Your Picture

It is indeed a subject of controversy. And you can find plenty of material online suggesting what type of picture you should use to represent you on LinkedIn. I advocate for social posts on the network as you will see later in the book, but for your main avatar in the network, you will need to respect a few rules.

The people not connected with you will see your picture. It will be seen on LinkedIn's search results, and it will be seen as a suggested connection to other people in your industry. And you want to make a good first impression. As human beings, we judge, and we judge hard. Our protective instincts do that for us. So let's play with it and make it natural for people to validate you Let's give them a nice close-up picture with white background and light, lots of light. You don't need to invest in a professional photo with an excellent camera in our pocket. You need to invest time in taking a great picture. I will tell you how now.

Do it during the day. Indoor but at the window where the sunlight hits. Find a way to place your phone on top of a cabinet or if you have a tripod or some of those selfie sticks that would work perfectly. Put the flash off and the timer as you want to go hands-free. Smile. I can't stress that enough, but don't be too serious in your picture unless your business is a Morgue. Your torso and face should cover 75% of the background. Don't be too close to the wall as you want to prevent shadows.

You will dress accordingly. You will dress for the position you want to get it. Remember, you are being judged, and even if that sounds scary for you, you can't avoid being judged so show them your best self. When you dress think about the contrast. You will avoid white blouses and shirts that won't create a contrast with the white background and your outfit. If you are using a dark or grey background, you might have issues with shadows, but you can still try a few angles until you get it. This will take some of your time, but it will be worth it, trust me. And your mobile phone will make the picture with a high resolution.

If you are taking the effort to have a beautiful picture, I am assuming that you won't use things like you and your kids, pets or you at the Bahamas (unless you are in Tourism.) You won't use pictures of you partying, drinking or riding a bike. Lifestyle sells a lot, but your static and "evergreen" picture must create trust, remember that.

And like I suggested the header background that can use a real picture of you in action (on stage, on a meeting, or on your desk), the same applies here for your avatar. But please make sure that your face is seen behind a microphone or your laptop monitor. Objects will play well in the image only if they are directly related to what you do. If used wisely, they will enhance your reach. People love connecting with people who they believe can bring them opportunities, though you might be in the same boat now, things will change soon, I am your biggest fan now.

For years I used a professionally produced picture taken in a Studio (I paid another photographer to do it as part of the branding we wanted to enforce to all of our associates.) That was nice because I had the same picture on all networks, and this immediately put me "in the map." This is something that you must do as well. Once you have your new picture, you will use the same picture on your Facebook, Twitter, Instagram, etc. I hope that by now you are convinced that you should be using all the networks to attract you good things the way I did.

Recently I decided to change my pictures to a set of pictures of me on stage. They were meticulously chosen to display me with the microphone in my hand, part of a screen in the background, and a strange face to show that I was making a point. In a matter of days have changed my picture, more and more connections and invitations to speak appeared. New prospects came to us, and the business thrived. Funny thing how things work nowadays. I imagine how difficult would have been to be invited to speak ten years ago based on a reputation created on face-to-face engagements and interactions. Kudos to the ones who were able to pull this off without the use of Social Media.

Your Tagline

That is one of the most exciting aspects of my methodology, and it will be a significant shift in the way you think about yourself and your brand. It is incredible how such a small number of characters combines can make that effect on people. As we discussed before, perhaps the fact that we need to grab the attention of people quickly in the first seconds of interaction does that with us. And we will play with it. We will play with that by going "all-in" and telling them what the value we bring to the table straight away is. There is an entire chapter dedicated to this topic so I won't go too deep in it right now. But I want you to think about this expensive Real Estate of your LinkedIn profile now.

The Tagline (or Headline) is that limited character space underneath your picture on LinkedIn. Most LinkedIn profiles will have this customised by the tool itself as they grab the current or past job position you had and fill the space with whatever you wrote in there. You might not know that you can customise that so I am here to tell you that yes you can, and yes you must. And you will be thoughtful when deciding what to include in the text line that defines you for the people who know you and for the people who don't.

Your Tagline will be brought together with your new picture when people find you scrambled with other profiles in the search results on LinkedIn. Your Tagline will be shown along with your picture on the board of suggested connections when people finalise their connections with other LinkedIn profiles. It will also appear in another board of recommended connections on the right bottom part of your Timeline. And it will be displayed to the people you will try to connect before they connect with you. Therefore they

AS HUMAN BEINGS, WE JUDGE. SO LET'S PLAY WITH IT AND MAKE IT NATURAL FOR PEOPLE TO VALIDATE YOU.

can judge by the sentence you wrote whether or not they connect with you.

A written sentence about what you do and what is the value you bring to the person you are trying to connect will have a way better effect than writing that you work for the company "ABC" or "XYZ." It will appeal better than being "Open to Opportunities" as the judging person will think that if they cannot give you an opportunity or if they don't want you soliciting to them they should not connect back to you. It is about building a relationship rather than bagging. It is about creating rapport and curiosity rather than being mediocre. It is about impressing people on the one-tenth of a second when they are judging you. Let's get back to it in depth later in the book.

You Summary

If you have limited room on your Tagline, in the Summary part of your LinkedIn you will have way more space to write. It is meant to be explored, yet, I see so many people underusing this precious space. Most people won't take the time to depict their story and keep that alive with recent happenings and achievements. Most people will jot down a few bullet points and mention that they have "attention to detail" when they are openly displaying their limited thought by displaying limited writing capabilities. So lame. If this is your case, perhaps that is the reason why you are open to opportunities now, and you could not see the opportunity that LinkedIn is giving you right there: To write about yourself.

So go there and tell the world your story. Tell them how you started and how you came to be the best Data Analyst or Civil Engineer in the region. Go there and tell them why you took time off to dedicate time to motherhood (or explain that this wasn't time off at all.) Lead the reader through your career transition and why you thought that studying Law in addition to being in the Finance will set you apart and give you an advantage over professionals who only have Finance in their background. People like stories, therefore you want to capture their attention (again) by writing something interesting right there in the first paragraph that will be shown when they visit your profile. And if you want to get extra motivation to write about yourself, think that every word you type in the Summary field on your LinkedIn profile is indexed and associated with your name. If I wrote "Personal Branding" in my summary, LinkedIn is associating this with "Felipe Lodi" in their database. And writing a few bullet points about your "Resilience" won't differentiate yourself. Much more to it on the dedicated chapter about your story.

Your Career Path

There are many discussions about whether or not

you should a have a long CV. You will listen to the opinions of Recruiters who will tell you to keep it short and concise, and you will listen to the views of Recruiters who will tell you to detail your career as much as you can. The bottom line is that they don't get a conclusion either. Agency Recruiters will like your long CV so that their parsing software will extract more keywords and a the better the chances are that you will be a good match (you didn't think that they read your CV, didn't you? They are in sales not in Human Resources.) In-house Recruiters will tell you to keep it short so that they won't stay after five reading your CV to see if you are a good fit for their culture.

I come from a country, and I have been noticing the same pattern in other countries in South America, where you work as you graduate. Yes, in Brazil you need to work during the day and study at night so that you can pay for your studies. And nobody dies from that. But as a result, when you get to your forties, you could have over thirty jobs in your history, especially if you are part of a trendy market that enables short-term contracting and freelancing. On the other hand, if you are a Freelancer or an Entrepreneur, you will want to describe your portfolio of successful projects and initiatives, and if you use a CV for that, you will quickly end up with a six-pages document like me.

The good news is that LinkedIn will enable that. And you must describe every little job you had since you sold lemonade on the corner of your street (well, that could be featured in your summary instead.) But my point is that you won't depend as much on the Recruiters to find opportunities now with the proper use of LinkedIn. Therefore, you should not consider what they tell you. The method I bring here will attract you opportunities, remember? You want to use your network to engage in conversations that will inform you about a position here, a client's need there, and whether or not your CV has six pages won't matter much when you are shortcutting your way through professional success.

Your career path must be detailed on LinkedIn. You must link your past jobs with the company pages of the companies you worked for, and you must put the dates. Don't be too preoccupied in writing the accurate month you left or started. If you had a little gap or two, fill those with the time you were interviewing for that particular job since you were already working for them without knowing. Don't be caught up by details that don't matter much. Be precise, though, when listing your responsibilities and key achievements because this is the information that will help you tell your successful story, build your Tagline from it and catch the eyes of the increased number of readers you will have after applying the method in this book.

You will create two headers for each job position you are listing: Responsibilities and Key

Achievements. Feel free to write a paragraph or two under each header, but my experience says that this is where you should be using the bullet points. Write the responsibilities in the infinitive and your achievements in the past. Be specific and be bold. You will need to think and catch up with your memory to remember every little detail of accomplishment. You will mention numbers, even if those numbers mean that a product or a method you implemented put people out of jobs. You are writing this to your future employer, therefore, if you are telling them that you have a way of automating a process and getting rid of ten people they will like you. If you are in Sales, cite the targets hit, or even if you got close to them, this is still remarkable. If you are in Health, spending your nights in the Emergency Room or caring for the elderly, describe how many cases in average you dealt. Get to be known by what you achieved even if you believe that these achievements are ordinary of your profession. They won't sound ordinary to other people. If you are in IT, you want to mention that you were coding but also giving a hand to the Data guys so that they could produce their dashboards. This will be listed as an achievement, and the readers will be able to understand that even though that wasn't your responsibility, you were running the extra mile. That plays way better displaying that you are a "Team Player" rather than saying in the Summary field that you are a team player. Facts tell more about you than you claiming a specific label to yourself.

Don't copy from your job description the responsibilities you had. Even if you have to keep it short, don't go there to the Website of the company you used to work to get what they do and apply to your profile. I have seen that, believe me. It is incredible how people can be lazy even when they need to describe themselves. Creating the habit of writing will benefit yourself in the long-term. I have a friend who says that writing is a marketable skill, everybody needs to do it. It will be difficult at first. Words won't come up easily, you will struggle, but it will be so worthy. In the company, we have a team of professionals trained to write about other people, and it is amazing how they can write about a person they just met. This is only possible because, during the career assessment they make, we scrutinise their history and make questions that will extract the best from them. You can do that too. Ask yourself what your primary responsibility in that specific job was. Answer this question first and notice how your brain will do the work of connecting facts that weren't in your recent memory. It is all there, you need to pull his off, and the words will come.

The best part of writing detailed information about your career path is that you also will improve your speech and storytelling about yourself. You will keep those facts in your recent memory, and that will help you incredibly on face-to-face and virtual conversations. That will help you with ideas for creating content about your industry and posts that will require only text. There is an entire chapter about content in this book, and you will see that posts containing only texts are the ones that bring the higher number of views. You will need to be creative and real, and it will be an incredible and useful exercise scanning through your profile and triggering your brain to tell a story about the day that you had to cover for your boss in a meeting with the Japanese. Trust me; storytelling is what you will have as the best ally in generating trust and increasing your network. You will learn how to tell stories full of subliminal messages about what you can do for your next client or employer. It is the selling without selling, thought the use of content, remember? The vehicle.

Your Contact Details

I watched a video from a self-called LinkedIn specialist on my timeline that suggested that you should not disclose your Email address on the contacts section of your profile. What? It is the opposite in my most profound belief. You must reveal your Email address, your Twitter account, Facebook, Pinterest, Instagram and your Grandmother's phone number if you can. Being accessible is one of the critical elements of your brand, and you must spend every hour of your day signing that you are available to people. The way you want to be contacted might not be the way that your client or future boss want to reach out to you. Make that convenient for them by displaying multiple contact options. Even the ones that are not ideal for you. It is about them and showing a link to your Twitter account even if you don't use Twitter will tell at least that you have nothing to hide. Is your Facebook still for Family and Friends only? Silly you. Go there and change the privacy of those post of you partying (everybody parties), make a few useful posts public and then past the address to your Facebook profile on your LinkedIn. Unprotect your Instagram account right now, or else your next client may think that you are involved in the Deep Web. Then paste all these addresses in the contacts section of your LinkedIn profile.

Your phone number must be there also. And don't forget that people won't know that your country code is 001 because you are based in the United States, don't assume that. Not including the country code not only limits your reach but also sends a message that you are presumptuous in thinking that everybody must know that the US uses 001. Got my point here? It is about being "truly" accessible. Humble yet global. Your phone number does not belong to you. It is just a tool that you must let it work for you. Of course, you will develop fame, and you don't want people bothering you as much, but in the beginning, you are most likely to be on the other side and displaying your phone number in the network is a clear sign of accessibility. You wouldn't know how this can make the difference when an opportunity needs to hit you. You must give convenience to the people who want to reach you, and making them scroll your profile or your other Social networks in search of your phone number when they want to give you a call rather than emailing you is the chance that you are providing them to get distracted by something else while they seek your phone number. The opportunity is gone.

Finally, don't worry about hackers and parsing mechanisms that will spam you with "Mobile Apps" Emails from India. You Email does not belong to you either. I can't stress that enough. It belongs to Google, or Yahoo, or Microsoft and it is hosted in a Datacenter somewhere around the globe, and you don't have control over it. Therefore use it as an assistant. Expose it to your benefit and let the messages come in. Filter or automate the filters to give you only what is useful and make sure that your accessibility will work as another selling point of your profile. I have seen people in Sales not displaying their phone number. People in Digital Marketing not displaying their Facebook account. People job hunting not displaying their Gmail account. Then they complain that the opportunities are not coming.

However, Email communication is doomed. We are living in the age of brief and fast communication. No one reads long Emails as we used to do in the past.

No wonder why more and more you don't get answers to your Emails. It is because you are probably not writing what matters on either the subject line or on the first sentence of your message (so that the readers will see what your message is about on their mobile notifications and without having to open the actual message.) Therefore, modern messaging is turning to asynchronous video and voice messages on WhatsApp or Facebook Messenger, and, if the message is long and needs interaction, the phone calls are back to the game.

So you guessed, in a rank of communication channels that you must put on your LinkedIn profile the top of the list is your Phone Number, then your WhatsApp, Messenger, Facebook, Instagram and Twitter Accounts. They are efficient and excellent communication tools. Becoming obsolete are your Email address and Skype account, yet, don't waste the opportunity to have them all displayed. If you must use your Email, follow up with a LinkedIn message to let them know that you emailed them. I do what I call the threefold communication. When I call a person that must get my message, I follow up with an Email message with better contents to what has been spoken over the phone, usually a contract, or commercial references or link to portfolio or brochures, and finally a text message on their LinkedIn profile to let them know that I either tried to call them or thanking for the chat.

THE WAY YOU
WANT TO BE
CONTACTED MIGHT
NOT BE THE WAY
THAT YOUR CLIENT
OR FUTURE BOSS
WANT TO REACH
OUT TO YOU.

My teams respect the following rules regarding communication: Emails are important but not urgent. If the message needs to be received immediately and act upon it is also expected, we use WhatsApp groups for broadcast to all the parties involved even if the message is aimed at a single person. If it is extremely urgent, or sometimes, even, a text message caused some discomfort, only a phone call (not a voice message) will solve the problem. These asynchronous communication tools are great but they are yet to transmit emotion, and nothing will replace the realtime phone call. That is effective communication, proven to work within my team. Taking this to yourself, think that the mere fact of displaying all of your communication channels will tell your future employer or client that you praise for collaboration. Point for you.

Your Files

On LinkedIn, you can upload and display all sorts of files on your profile. Your diplomas, certifications, your CV in Word format, your sales presentations, your company brochures, designs, sketches, your college paper, published article, eBooks, thesis and dissertations. It is like if you had a blank canvas for your creations that will validate what you wrote, whatever that is. Imagine putting together with your sales numbers, as one of your key achievements for a determined past job, the reports and dashboards showing your name and the logo of the company you used to work. I wouldn't worry much about copyrights here if you believe that the information is not too sensitive. The company will feel somehow rewarded by having you display their achievements together with yours. If you are a researcher, for example, a chemist or a sociologist, why isn't your thesis uploaded to LinkedIn? Will you let this get rotten in the University library or somewhere in your hard drive (if you still know where that is.) And what about that nice PowerPoint presentation you built to onboard forthy new employees on the factory you used to work as a Human Resources Associate? Where is it? See? Perhaps the fact you don't even know where your files are, files that were once very important for you justifies the fact that you are not using LinkedIn to its full potential. Let's address that. I am here with you.

You can, and you must, be exploring the fact that you can upload your videos too. I know, I got you scared now, regretful for being acquired this book. I am too scared of making videos too, and I have been making them for a little while now. You need to trust me when I say that from the moment you hit "Record" on your first ever video it only gets better and better. You get better; your posture improves, your thoughts get more meaningful, your attitude towards the camera gets natural as you go. There is no way to get worse once you took the courage to push your limits by entering this incredible video movement. You will feel occur, at first, until you reap the rewards of displaying on video what you cannot show on paper. Your body language improves as you keep filming yourself, your speech, your vocabulary and your confidence to enter rooms, meetings, parties, gatherings, and you guessed, interviews.

You will be approaching this heavily when we talk about creative content creation in this book. And I will give you so many reasons to finish this book and start starring the show that will bring so many benefits to yourself, on the personal and professional sides. By now, since we are still building your new profiles, what I need you to think is about what video material can you upload to LinkedIn. I am asking you to check your hard drive for footage of you speaking or on meetings, or participating in conferences, etc. Don't stop building your profile if cannot get anything in this regard. I am only asking that if you have it, put it on. LinkedIn will also accept links to platforms such as YouTube and Vimeo. Therefore you don't need to own the piece of video to use it on your profile.

We recently opened a few positions of our Learning and Development programmes that will lead IT professionals to work with the European Commission in Brussels, Belgium. I went there and recorded two five minutes pieces telling why people should apply. I recorded two videos, one in English and another in Portuguese, my mother tongue. I went through, in one shot, explaining why we are collaborating with a few companies in Belgium for these positions and I posted the videos on Facebook, LinkedIn, Twitter and Instagram (well, I can tell you that Europe is suffering by the lack of talent, in all industries.) At the end of the videos, I proposed to the candidates that they recorded their videos stating why they should be considered to our programmes and for a chance of being considered to work for the European Commission. Not only weren't we accepting boring paper CVs (though people insisted in sending us that) but we wanted to evaluate the level of English, posture and courage for recording their content. Kind of "I want this so bad that I am going to push my limits" approach. To being with, we are not a Recruitment Agency, and we also fight against their malpractices at the European level, therefore if we were jointly participating in an initiative that would resemble a recruitment process, my first thought and an easy one was what could we do to set the tone to people that only the best ones will be selected. As of September of 2018, the campaign is still on, and we have received a few recorded material in addition to static online applications and a group of people who didn't bother to watch the five minutes video to see the catch. We didn't read their CVs either.

I can't deny that I was inspired by the American Grant Cardone, who is known, in addition to being an extraordinary salesperson, to recruit their people by asking candidates to record their forty-five seconds' videos explaining why they should work with him. Amazing. Why aren't all industries using this approach? You can get so many things from a short video like that. That is fine if the video is followed by a Word CV or a link to a LinkedIn profile, but the short video will display conciseness, speech, language skills, body language, presentation, clothing, organisation and the fact that if the person had the stones to get in front of the camera, hit record and send, there won't be a challenge that this person won't overcome. Simply put.

So why don't you set yourself apart from the immense majority of people who are not doing this yet? Markets are turning more and more demanding, and you must think about doing something bold to catch the attention of your audience. You don't have an audience yet, I know, but attitudes like that, recording your pieces of content, will bring you the audience. From your audience, your network will increase, and from your increased network, your opportunities will arise. When the opportunities come, you will feel prepared merely because you self-prepared recording the videos that you used to get to this point in the first place.

Your Tagline Isn't
Where You Work

I bet you're thinking about the risk of using something new and being bold on the network. I will tell you that this is what this book is all about it. Being different and audacious. I will keep telling you that throughout the book because that is what I believe. Not only am I proof that this brings results, but I am also a natural advocate of "escaping the bubble." I lived this life for years and years. As the IT professional who grew baby steps and made a living, I was in my comfort zone. I never kept quiet where I worked, though, but concerning Social Media, I had always taken a conservative approach. Partly because I left Brazil and succeed abroad, I didn't want to show the people still there that winning does not require a finish line. I remember winning when I rang my wife to tell her that I had a passport renewed ten years ago before boarding the British Airways flight to move to Belgium. That meant a lot to me. I wish I had documented it all using the Social Media. I never had the profile of a "bragging person." But now I realised that bragging is a thing, and those who don't use it, are left behind.

We follow these celebrities online. And most of them have never starred Hollywood movies. They become celebrities for play what I call "Bragging Marketing." They fly private, ride a Ferrari and speak on stage to 3000 people. The latter resonates better to me than material things. We can deny how powerful showing off is, and how the Internet and the Social

Media are taken by it nowadays. It is giving people what they want. On a daily basis, people fall short on selling themselves. They can pitch what they do, most of them cannot even go beyond the term coined by society to label what they do. I am Developer; I am a Nurse, I work with Events. So lame. Put some more adjectives to it and the value you bring to the table, and you got yourself a Tagline. Or a Headline as called on LinkedIn.

So I ask: Why aren't you bold when explaining what you do? You are faced with this question way more than you might think. You are presented with this question when you need the strengths to exercise in the morning. You are presented with this question when someone small talks with you in the elevator. You are presented with this question when you meet a new person when waiting for your kid to finish her Judo class. If you want to be labelled and belong to a group or a class of professionals, you will be limited to the salaries they get and to the list of leads of people who downloaded your eBook from your Website. A label will limit you; a Tagline will widen your horizons. You will see their eyebrows raise when you deliberately say that you "make a company save" or that "you save lives for a living." Bold, isn't it? It is another approach.

It took me a while for being in a position to write a book, especially about LinkedIn. But you probably realised by now that LinkedIn was an excuse for motivating and inspiring you. LinkedIn is the backdrop that I needed for putting you, professional, in a position of prominence that will bring you the confidence and the opportunities you deserve. Because you are good at what you do, I know you are. You only need to tell that to the world. And LinkedIn is the best professional tool there is. Use it with no moderation and let everyone know what you do best. I am in a position to say that now because of the number of people I got to jobs in Europe because of my LinkedIn strategy. And it is funny to see that the people who didn't succeed in our programme come back to the former boring Tagline they had as if this was the cause that they didn't achieve. I thank them for their trust in the first place but thank even more for the fact they helped me understand the behaviour that drags down people to fail: The fear.

The power of a Tagline that stands out is contagious. It is the first thing that I advise a person when they come to me for a freebie. I help another person succeed, it does not cost me nothing, and I sharpen my thoughts the more I create Taglines "on-the-fly." The Influencers who teach and motivate the subscribers of our programmers also customise their Taglines. It is beautiful to see things like "I lead the most amazing international team...", "I am a career builder with over ten years of experience...", "I manage next-generation PMOs..." or "I coach professionals, teach university students and voluntarily assist children with special needs." These are only a few examples of meaningful Taglines our Influencers use instead of "Team Leader", "Human Resources Specialist", "Project Manager" or "Teacher." See the difference? I bet you still belong to the team of Tagline losers, don't you? But this will change, I know it will.

We depicted the ideal format for your profile that fits into the creative content strategy that we will see soon. I don't recommend, but if you must deviate from what I suggested you on that chapter, please do not use boring terms on your Tagline or bullet points on your summary, I beg you. The Tagline is the most expensive Real Estate of your profile that you play to your benefit even when you are not connected to people. Don't waste the opportunity to use keywords that you help you be found but in a sentence that makes sense to the reader. Though we spoke about your career path, we are now talking about your Tagline, and we will discuss your summary in depth, you must leave the Tagline for last. Like the title of a book or a song. Leave to the end so that you will have a comprehensive understanding of what you are and what is the value that you bring (and brought) to the table through the years.

Ok. You just left college and are reading this book, and I am talking about career path while you are still chasing your first shot. Another reason for you to be bold, my friend. If you took the Academic route (I did it too), you would be playing with sentences like "I am the first Researcher of Trinity's College in Ireland to find that...", "I authored the A-graded paper...and I now want to work for the private sector." or "I am a natural Team Leader and organised the 2018's Summer Games of..." You go figure. What did you do that was meaningful? Your Tagline not necessarily needs to infer that you made someone gets richer to attract the eyes of people who can get you an opportunity. But you don't go there and say that you are "Open to opportunities" to a market that is turning more demanding every day. Don't mix bagging with bragging.

It is my role here, though, to make things easier for you. I want very badly to see this becoming a trend. The age of the bold people. The time when people nearly hang a billboard to their necks to advertise what they do best. Therefore I will describe what components the ideal Tagline must have. You must explore your problem-solving skills on top of all. You must also explore the fanciest term of your industry to impress people. And you can explore things like geographic locations if you want to narrow your opportunities to a specific place in the Globe (or in Mars if you're going to work for Elon Musk.) LinkedIn viewers will stop scrolling or hovering their eyes upon your Tagline and your beautiful new picture at the moment they interpret a term they relate. And then they read it all and create a judgment about you. The judgment will come in the form of a

USE YOUR TAGLINE WITH NO MODERATION AND LET EVERYONE KNOW WHAT YOU DO BEST.

criticism (good), it will come in the form of curiosity (better), it will come in the form of a praise (much better), it will generate a click on your profile (that you can track) and it will create a new connection if the viewer feels like they can either benefit from you or give you an opportunity. Excellent side effects that you generated by being bold enough to tell the world what you do best.

You are now wondering what your "Civil Engineer", "Open to Opportunities", "European Citizen" or "LION Networker" ever brought you. Don't worry; nothing is lost, there is still time for you to improve. Do you want to change? Start with the pronoun "I", that is an easy one. Think now of a verb that impresses people right there on the spot. Do you want an easy one? Go for "Help." (Well, you will need if you cannot think of a verb that illustrates better what you do.) It is also perfectly fine to call yourself the Specialist or the Expert. But make sure that you specialise in what you do because people will make you questions and start conversations that will demand answers from you as the specialist you are.

On our Workshops and Conferences, especially when I get to this topic, I put a formula in the screen that says: "I Help + ABC + get + XYZ"), and then I throw at the screen a few real-life examples as I took from our Influencers. I use the verb "Help" to smoothly trigger their brains to come up with some more robust such as "I Increase...", "I Build...", "I Change..." or "I

Organise..." If I give these verbs to them, they think that they cannot come up with anything better. These are simple combos that work because they imply leadership and control over something, and leadership are the most well-positioned skill set nowadays. If you are showing right there in your Tagline that you might be the leader that they are looking for, good, it will work. Don't get caught up in saying that you "manage a team." You manage systems and processes; people are not managed, they are led. Therefore, make sure that your Tagline is not showing a dark side of you that will refrain opportunities to hit you instead.

Keep moving to what you increase, build, change or organise, according to the examples above, and connect to a significant and powerful word that will keep people with you. "I Increase the Sales...", "I Build Custom Systems...", "I Change your Internal Process..." or "I Organise your Paperwork..." It is getting better and better, isn't it? We are getting to it, together. I will be there with you through the end. And now? Sales of what? What type of Custom Systems, Internal Processes? What do you mean by Paperwork? Let's be more specific. The specification will narrow will down; you are drilling into your audience and the audience that you don't have yet. "I Increase the Sales of your Real Estate...", "I Build Custom SharePoint Systems...", "I Change your Internal Accounting Processes..." or "I Organise the Paperwork of your Mortage Application..." Nearly there now. You will need now to explain how you do those things, and if you must, put some geographic information in your Tagline to narrow your opporunities to that location. "I Increase the Sales of your Real Estate in Miami by Enabling Long Term Loans for the Down Payment", "I Build Custom SharePoint Systems from Two to Four Weeks", "I Change your Internal Accounting Processes by Moving to Integrated SaaS" or "I Organise the Paperwork of your Mortgage Application and Guarantee 90% of Approval."

These are all bold and arrogant Taglines. The way that is guaranteed to attract people to your profile. You have the keywords as well (though LinkedIn won't depend only on these keywords to position you.) You have the location and positive words, you display the professional that you are, and this is what they will get if they hire you or buy your product. Did you notice that I capitalised the important words? You must, for readability purposes. It must, and it will look like a copywriting taken from an Apple product. That is how you must look at yourself from now on. As the unique product and not as a commodity labelled like everyone else.

Storytelling Makes You Credible

What's your story? That is the question that I make to most people from whom I accept connections in LinkedIn. It is incredible and worrying about how people cannot put together a few lines about themselves. Of course, I must disregard my statistics about the number of people who don't reply to that at all. I instead believe that they are either busy or missed the call for a conversation than they cannot write about themselves. Are you compelled to tell your story? Well, you should. People love stories, and there is no better way to relate than putting off your challenges through life, your recent motivations and telling the world how you came to be what you are today. And here is why I believe that most people won't write their own stories: the fear of being judged. At the moment you figure that you are writing for a small and specific group of people, you will lose the restraints and your words will flow naturally. Your story is unique to the world. The people you met through life, the work you had, the problems you solved and the things you learned, only "you" have this combination that makes you unique. Play with it. Play with these specifications that you once believed had to value to people. You are wrong to think that the fact that you studied Law in college and then moved to IT is not attractive to people whereas the fact that you are in IT with a background in Law makes you excellent for writing technical contracts for a big consultancy. But people must know your story first.

The job market nowadays is made of specific roles. Yes, I know that must of you are the "Jack of all trades", and that you would love to tell the world that you do from A to Z. But the market doesn't want that. They want your specification. They want the medical device specialist. They want the Coder of that rare programming language. They want the Finance Analyst who is an expert in Bonds of the German Stock Market. But that doesn't mean that you won't be the "do it all" because you must too. But you won't use this to sell yourself. Your story should tell the reader how you became the unique professional, and intelligently mention all the other skill sets you have that led you to become the specialist. Once you sit on that nice desk in your new office, then you will unveil all the features of the product "You."

Bear in mind, though, that you must not be so comfortable in your new desk felling that you found your dream job for life. Companies don't want you to stick around that long anymore. They want to put together the right talent for a specific project and then see if you can be of any use on another project later on. Talent, though required, are detachable. And you must think of yourself in that way too. You must believe from day one on a new job, what will your next project be. What country you will be working on, and what skill sets you will be plugging to your utility belt. Be mindful when telling your story that a frequent change of jobs and companies must be illustrated as a progressive and natural career path. You were growing and accumulating experiences and not being left aside and pushed from one company to the other. You chose where to be and even if you took the wrong direction in the past, let everybody think that you knew what you were doing and that you are not afraid of making mistakes. Mistakes that brought you where you are now, mistakes that made you unique.

In the company, we started to write the stories of people on LinkedIn. The Storytelling is a strong selling point of our product. I will any day soon, put another book together with the stories written about the people we branded. I like so much the particularities of each story that, I launched in Ireland a franchise of live events called Young Success Stories that told in several opportunities the perseverance tales of the Brazilians living in the Emerald Island. They cleaned the toilets and served coffees until they found their way through networking and exposure to big corporations and successful businesses. Their stories resonated so well that together with Gerard Bissett, a talented young Irish author, we launched a book with their transcripted stories told at the events.

People love stories, and they will enjoy yours too. So why aren't you telling your story on LinkedIn? It is tricky, though, to understand that the Summary part of your profile should be dedicated to your tale, so most people will put boring bullet points and a

YOU MUST NOT
BE COMFORTABLE
IN YOUR NEW
WORK FELLING
THAT YOU FOUND
YOUR DREAM
JOB. COMPANIES
DON'T WANT YOU
TO STICK AROUND
THAT LONG
ANYMORE.

single paragraph exaggerating about what they are. I know. You did that too. And now, I will convince you that underusing this another expensive Real Estate on your profile is a big mistake for a few reasons. When you jot down just a few words about yourself, you are sending a message to the viewers of your profile that you are lazy. That you don't have the writing skills needed to nearly every qualified job there is. And that you couldn't put together, in a storytelling manner, why you are unique and opted to put random words about yourself that have no meaning. There is no point on telling people that you are "Organised" if you are not writing "...in my first week with that company, I was able to establish new processes that would reduce in 25% the paperwork dealt by the clerk." See the difference here? See what I just did to tell the readers that you are organised?

Storytelling is an ageless strategy to get people's attention. It is when you have the opportunity to talk without being interrupted. It is when you have the stage to your monologue. It is when you are confident enough to describe both your wins and losses. It is when you make people trust in you. It is for everyone. Never believe that you cannot write. And believe in me when I tell you that the only thing that you need to do is to put distractions aside and start with the first sentence. Imagine that you are talking to a friend. You will struggle with the English as I did, but you will use helpers such as spelling and grammar correctors until you get the confidence to accelerate the process of writing.

The challenge here, though, is to write your story on your LinkedIn. For that, you will need extra help from the career path you will put together as part of your new profile build. This will be your guide and what will make you remember facts from the past. You will reuse elements from that and even repeat a few lines if needed. But instead of using the bullet points, recommended for that part of your profile, you will put your responsibilities and key achievements mixed in your story. Making sense and connecting your life facts in a way that the reader will want to finish and understand more about you. At first, don't be too concerned with the structure as you will dedicate time to review it. You can either begin by telling how you started to present times or by describing what you want right now to the beginning of your story. If you feel compelled to expose that you need an opportunity to shine, your story is the best way for you to sell yourself, not on your Tagline. If you just left College and you want you are chasing your first shot, you will start by saying "I never thought that I could write 10,000 words in my dissertation. I was able to prove why the Middle-class in Germany is shrinking to give birth to a new class called..." Aren't you compelled to read what I have to say? That is the effect that you want to bring to your Summary field on LinkedIn. That plays better than saying "Recently graduated in Sociology, looking for my first opportunity in the field...blah!"

Be Bold and Overvaluate your Achievements

Nobody will understand what you want better than you. Nobody will give the value you deserve for past achievements unless you tell them to do so. You must be bold when describing your progress through life with a bit of exaggeration too. You must be presumptions and link wise adjectives to your persona. No one else will do for you until you become a recognised brand. Besides, people will perceive you the way that you want as long as you tell them the right story. Therefore, your story must contain in every sentence elements that will keep the reader impressed even if that means surprising former colleagues with the fact that you said that you were "the best Financial Analyst of the team." You won't claim achievements that weren't yours, of course, but if you belonged to a team that together doubled the sales of the "North division" you will brag and be vague about who did what in your team.

You will learn the thin line between tweaking people's perception and distorting the reality without breaking your character. Becoming a brand on LinkedIn and being criticised might bring you a few foes, but you will be the excellence to the majority. When writing your story, you will be required to continually analyse your acts and behaviours, assuming that the viewers will have a way of understanding you. As human beings, we judge all the time. I judge all the time. Judging helped me write this book. Because I am not afraid to be judged anymore. As soon as you trigger this on you, and I am here for you on this mission, you will realise that you can write about yourself, fearless, genuinely believing in things such as "I am the first LinkedIn author in Ireland, and I am now claiming monopoly in the Learning and Development field with the sudden launch of my book." That is pretty much the truth. When everyone else is concerned about what people will think about them, and whether or not they should use a different type of online engagement, you will be writing a killer LinkedIn profile that will change the perception people have about you.

Should you write on the third person? Hell, yes! Especially if you want to give the impression that you paid someone to write that for you; That you invested in a professional writing service to get that beautiful picture of yours painted and published professionally. The Recruiters will complain, the Salespeople in disguise who know nothing about personal development. And you will stick strongly when they criticise you. That means that it is working. Keep pushing.

Should you write in the first person instead? Hell, yes! Being bold and presumptions on the first person will have an even better effect on people. When they read things like "I was awarded the best Java Programmer in the West Coast." You didn't think to keep quiet, didn't you? Go there and claim your spot. The world needs people who are bold in their achievements, meaningful stories must be told, and yours is no different than mine. The only difference is that you haven't told that yet because you were too afraid to be judged. If you for a second believed that this book would bring a recipe to the ordinary, you were wrong. I promise you that if you execute every step in this book, step through the content creation, as you will see in the next chapters. Get to the point of collaborating with people on conversations, groups and company pages, effectively and constantly. I promise you that many opportunities will arise. You cannot see them yet because seeing the big picture is not that easy. Many aspects are still hidden for you. I promise you that if you apply the teachings herein and you don't get a single opportunity, I will give your investment in this book back. That is my pledge to you, and I am not afraid of saying that.

Don't Let People Tell You That You Have a Gap

I have spoken about the "gap ghost" so many times. I know that people create this obstacle when they think about pursuing what they desire. I truly despise people who make excuses for themselves. A career gap is nothing. This is something that the Recruiters created to undervalue you. Don't fall for that. It is the same when a company requires a professional with "x" years of experience. This is so subjective, demanding that a person needs a specific number of years to nail a job whereas another professional with fewer years of experience can outperform the other. I cannot believe that in this day and age, we are still living by the rules established by the big corporations. I hope this book can shed some light at them.

The portfolio we deliver to people on our Learning and Development programmes is full of novelties. We do make the boring paper CV, but we keep all the information consistent with the one we put on their LinkedIn profiles. We headshot them and record their interviews on studio and edit everything to its perfection. Once we have their data compiled, we also design a set of advertisement artwork that we plug into weekly Marketing campaigns exposed to a large number of people on several Social Networks and Email lists. Such artwork displays their skills on charts and badges where we also accommodate their years of experience. I idealised all this material to bring convenience to any viewer, on any channel. Though I don't believe in raking people by their years of experience, I strongly believe that must praise for their years of experience. Let's not make a mix up here. One thing is you being grateful and hanging a badge on your chest saying that you have over twenty years of experience as a Nurse and the other is limiting a job position to Nurses with over twenty years of experience only. One could have been for twenty years working in a calm and quiet hospital in Oslo, Norway whereas the other could have been for five years serving with the Military in Afghanistan.

Therefore, if you are up for discussing and evaluating how to describe a specific gap in your career, I am with you because you are intended to overcome the challenge of writing. First, what is a gap? Unless you tell me that you got jailed or went on Sabbatical, what you believe is a gap is not a gap. Did you take time off the conventional nine-to-five work as maternity leave? Because that doesn't sound like a break to me. Moms are the best Project Managers that I have ever seen, isn't that right? And they are also into Nutrition, Logistics, Procurement and Health. They read about food; they multitask the Household finances while cooking and they find the best online deal for wipes and nappies while feeding their babies. And they still make themselves available for their husbands and maybe a few kids more added to the mix. Did you take time off to study English? Well, that was a challenge, and you feel now prepared to come back to work. Amazing! Record a video showing off your newly acquired language skills saying that you are back to the game. Congratulations, you are now part of a selective group of people who speak more than one language. Learn how to make the best of a situation that others judge as impeditive.

When my wife and I moved to Europe in 2008, I came with a job and a work permit granted by the Belgian authorities to work for a small IT company outside of Brussels, the capital. Our first challenge was to have her working in her area, Human Resources. We didn't know that they would require English, French and Dutch to occupy a desk in a corporation over there. Had we laid back and waited for an English-only opportunity to come to her, we would probably still be waiting for that to happen. We took the challenge on and enrolled her in English and French classes. In two years she became fluent on both, and she now speaks three languages. Was that a gap? If we had played the victim and allowed Recruiters to dictate what should happen to her, she would never become CFO of our companies and employed other people in Ireland. That after had stopped for another three years to take care of our daughter.

My message here is for you never allow people to label you. Invest in yourself and learn how to win an argument. I have seen people coming to Ireland and claiming their Work Permit to companies over the phone. Saying that they would work for free for a month so that they could prove their value. Always remember to practice the forefront attitude that you impress people immediately after you take the "I don't think so" hit. Insist over the phone, go to their offices, annoy people for a chance. They will believe that the same person who is fighting for their space will be competing for their company, advocating for their brand, exceeding targets and leading colleagues towards a common goal. It is a display, always a display.

Build Your Pitch

How do you pitch what you do? Have you done it at all? How do you develop your answer to that question "can you tell me more about yourself"? I want you to remember this for life now. Not only will people judge you but they will judge you in the first moments of interaction. Some natural protective mechanism, I believe we have, that will make us either trust or distrust a person we just met. Therefore, you must be bold, as we discussed, and the boldest part of your pitch must come at the beginning of it. In your first or in your second sentence, when people have their radars still on you. Keep that in mind.

The term "Pitch" is highly associated with

Sales. The Sales pitch. And there is a strong reason why we are using this word. I want you to think of yourself as a product. Have you noticed the TV advertisements lately? Have you noticed that they try to grab your attention during the first seconds? Notice how the brand or the name of the product come at the final seconds of the video. Professionals in this area understand well how to catch your attention and how to make their message remarkable. And you want to apply the same techniques they do. You can't afford to lose any opportunity to interact with people and leave an impression, a judgement or an opinion.

The big part of this book I wrote while on Holidays with the Family. Every day I woke up at 5 AM to make the best of my mornings without affecting the quality time that I had planned with them. I went to a special place in the hotel that I knew that would be opened during those hours, and that I would have a chance to have my first cup of coffee before breakfast was served to the guests. In this particular place, a man was catering only drinks for the guests that preferred enjoying their holidays until late hours. Coffee would have been complicated to get if it wasn't for the fact that I told the man behind the counter that I had my laptop on me because I was writing my book. I kept my story on explaining the reason behind me writing a book, and that this was important for positioning myself, and so. Useless. The man only remembered the fact that I was an author. Though I was still writing the book, I didn't sell myself short. And it was amazing how the man deliberately had the decision to serve me coffee assuming that I wasn't there for the drinks. I was there to work on my book, plain and simple. Guess how he remembers me now? I could have told him that I was an Astronaut and he would have believed in it. Keep playing this role would have been way more difficult than playing the author to the man.

You will see when we discuss the content creation that grabbing the attention of people starts with the compelling title that you use. The same way we applied the concepts on your Tagline that will make people read your profile and consequently connect with you. The title will tell the reader if the subject is for them. The same way that the first sentences of your pitch will tell the interlocutor if the chat will interest them. Play with that by bringing components from your story that fit in every situation. You will need to have all these thoughts" on the fly" as you interact with people. And depending on how you want to benefit from the conversation, you will keep bringing aligned and associated components to continue making an impression.

That is probably the main reason why you will write your story. Your story is not only for your LinkedIn once you have it. Your story will benefit you greatly when the conversations created through your online exposure happen. And yes they will happen. You must, and you will know your story better from now on. The writing of your new LinkedIn profile is just an excuse for that to happen. You will feel energised by your life achievements and grateful to have done it. You will see how people will relate to your story and make reference to it, even. I fell amazingly rewarded when I meet someone who tells me that they read my story on one of my articles online, or that they read my profile and know how I started and how I became to be an entrepreneur. I didn't see my story playing until I pushed hard with content, though. I learned that people would consume your content on their time when that suits them. They will get to a post you wrote before reading the second, the third and realising that you didn't go away. Then they look further. Or they will read your story first and create a relation between your life achievements and your fresh content online and say to you "I know where you are getting to with you recent campaigns. Is this because you lived in Brussels?" Little by little you will notice the results of your engagement on LinkedIn. If you keep consistency and if you are authentic, people will relate to you, and the opportunities will come. In the next chapter, I will tell you how I came to own a few companies and brands because of a guy whom I never met. That is what you heard.

KNOWING
YOUR STORY
WILL BENEFIT
YOU GREATLY
WHEN THE
CONVERSATIONS
CREATED
THROUGH YOUR
ONLINE EXPOSURE
HAPPEN.

The LION Networker is for The Losers

I am here to advise you, and I ask: Do you want 10,000 new followers from China right now? Nothing against our friends from the Eastern side of the globe but I guess you know that there is a black market on the Internet where you can buy Connections, Followers, Likes and Shares. They will look like you had them. And they won't come only from China, of course not, but they will be made of useless, and probably, fake logins that won't get you the real benefit of growing a network organically. What good will make you having three hundred Shares to connections that are not in your funnel? It is impressive to see a large number of followers on people's profiles, though. But when that doesn't match the level of notoriety that the person has, it looks fake and shallow. A LinkedIn profile cannot get to a large number of followers without constantly sharing value for a few years. Apart from public figures, you will notice that big networks are built based on a theme or on a type of message that stands out. A message that arouses and put people together.

Having the term "LION" anywhere on your LinkedIn profile signs to people that you are open to any type of connections. That you just don't care what these connections are about, and that you want to belong to any "Tribe." It looks desperate. Little do they know that LinkedIn itself has a resource to tell people that you are open to connections. It is way more elegant to use the feature than it is to belong to a group of people that first, doesn't create any compelling content surrounding their idea of "community", and second, most people will use the "LION" term on their Tagline. Together with their "Open to Opportunities" lame sentence. It is a waste of expensive Real Estate where you could be displaying your problem-solving Tagline. Besides, it is way more useful to have five hundred connections made of people who came through the content you post online than having the 10,000 followers that will hit your post randomly and never buy or hire from you.

Content Authoring on LinkedIn

Don't be afraid of the word "Content." You will find many definitions on the Web and guidance on how you should be creating content online. What they never consider, though, is that you are not an Author. You never wrote anything, and until now, you never thought of writing something that could resonate to people. And you never thought that this could bring you opportunities. Not as a Writer but in your industry. I am here to tell you that you don't need to become an Author to write, find and curate content that will show to your connections how you have been learning and progressing, and educating for free. Because the more content you will push online, the bigger will be the magic surrounding your profile. You want to be in every place, all the time so that people will remember about you when they hear keywords related to the content that you are posting online. That is the effect that you want to cause. Content is not "King" as Bill Gates once said. Content is your Kingdom. It will be the environment you will set to attract people with the same background, it will attract people who know someone with the same knowledge as you, and it will attract people who want to have the same experience as you. Ther reach is immeasurable. And I will show you how to do it and tell you a few stories that will convince you that you must be creating content online as a way to expose yourself. Opportunities will be thrown at you, and the only thing that you will need to do is to let them hit you.

My Content

For many years I was the IT guy. The developer, learned by myself how to programme a computer. In 1994, I started with Clipper and using only a thick book as a reference, and I built a system that was sold to over twelve hardware stores. The system was excellent and could work either on wholesale or retail. I had no experience with Sales, yet, I was the man pushing through referrals and making a living as the Young Entrepreneur. The Internet was only a baby, and Social Media wasn't there yet. Mobile phones didn't take pictures, and Digital Cameras had a huge slot for 3.5 disks that could transfer the images to a computer. That was a must. I wish I had documented all this to put that on my feeds. I wish I had shown people how my entrepreneurial instincts started twenty and some years ago.

The challenges were huge, and I gave up for a fixed salary working as a Junior Developer for a Seaport corporation in Brazil. I had the opportunity to learn new things, the process of delivering software for a few hundred users. I remember being very happy when wandering around the operations' offices and seeing all those people using another software I created. I wish I had a camera. I wish I had documented the fact that I grew to become a Senior Developer in a few years, moving from Brazil to Belgium regarded as a .NET Specialist, the company entitled me. I was living my years, and things were yet to improve.

Before I left Brazil, I was working for the Universal Music Group, and it was common to have people from European and American offices visiting us. One of the guys showed us a thing called "Facebook", and to me, that looked silly, and I would never give another thought to that. We went to a Soccer game in one of the nights, and one of the British guys was constantly taking pictures of the game and posting online. "What is the purpose", I thought. Facebook was there to stay, and I had no clue about it. What was closer to me, and my industry was the "blogging." Of course, as the developer that I was, Google was the perfect partner in helping me find that piece of code missing or the answer for that code that wasn't compiling. And then we had a few "Celebrities" that were the geeks who would put all that content online for free. Well, by then, they were all betting that creating an audience and selling advertisement afterwards would bring them extra cash. They were right, they started earlier than everyone else and benefited from building an audience that would read, like and share their stuff. And do you believe that the Ads they put on their Blogs were everything they got it? Of course not. If you track down these guys now, they are leading companies, or launched online products, or are paid for speaking gigs. The Content turned to gold. It paid off for them, Kudos to them.

I was never one of these guys because I was

lazy. I knew too much, enough for riding that wave, but I didn't. I was too afraid of being judged, afraid of not keeping up with the frequent content needed to leverage such platforms, fearful of the guys who knew more than me. I wish I had documented it all, but I don't regret because I had several other chances to start from scratch with my content. When doing my Masters of Internet Systems with the University of Liverpool, I was required to deliver two essays a week. The course was one hundred per cent online, and writing was taking too much of my time for good. I learned that I could write in English, which was awesome. And that writing was improving my speaking since I used the same brain mechanism for writing and speaking. The writing was increasing my vocabulary. English seems to have way more nouns than Portuguese, my mother tongue, and knowing how to diversify was paramount to my writing. The marks started to come above the average, so I knew that I was up to something, until I had the idea to start publishing my essays in a Blog. "Lodi Way of Learning" was the title. As the subjects of my articles surrounded the same themes, I had what I needed to start building my audience. Little did I know that the audience would not come from the readers but one single reader: the School Advisor who enrolled me in the course knew about my initiative and invited me to speak a few times at the online sessions of the University. I could describe my experiences and inspire students from all over the world to follow their Academic path. The Blog is discontinued now, but from that experience, I learned that my writing was more than satisfactory and that I could speak to the masses. I was several steps closer to something more significant and more meaningful to me. And I wasn't afraid anymore.

Opportunities are in disguise. Most people can't see that. Most of the time, you need to go through something that you thought that would be the opportunity itself to unveil an insight, a referral a connection that will lead you to the real opportunity. With the Social Media is no different. You will need to dig deeper. And the opportunities won't be in the job post, but in the connection made with the person who posted the job. It won't be in the new connection accepted but with the person connected with your new connection. It won't be the event you went to, but in the picture, you posted about the event. When you start having this mentality you don't give up. You won't waste another job application that you thought the requirements weren't for your skill set. You won't miss accepting another connection or the chance of posting your visit to the Museum. Social Media is not intended for fun, and all these networks that you believed were for "friends and family" can be widening your chances of success. The more you practice and explore them, the more you expose yourself.

SOCIAL MEDIA IS NOT INTENDED FOR FUN, AND ALL THE NETWORKS THAT YOU BELIEVED WERE FOR YOUR FRIENDS AND FAMILY CAN BE WIDENING YOUR CHANCES OF SUCCESS.

When I started using LinkedIn, I only had my profile up there. Like most of you, I bet. I remember the first post I did. It was something about how much coffee you have in a day and a relationship with your smartness. I was afraid of hitting that share button. Especially for the fact that it was a "Social" post, not directly related to my work or profession. That was somewhere in 2015. Not too long ago. I must admit that I am not one of the Dinosaurs of Social Media. And yes, you are reading a book of someone who has a little bit more of online exposure than you, or perhaps less. But my point is that the post about coffee was critical to me because it broke through what is nowadays a group of a few businesses and recognisable brands that surround my person and my leadership.

My partner and I were going through changes in the leading company as we wanted to turn the IT Consultancy into a Human Resources business. The natural route would be becoming another Recruitment Agency specialised in IT contractors, but we were never up to do more of the same. We wanted something that could dominate and not compete. What would have been the fun on having to keep looking at our competitors on our rearview mirror with absolutely no time to create or innovate in the market? So we decided to build a business to teach people to take the same steps we did to emigrate. We created services as products, built a Website and the company pages but the clients didn't come. We weren't known. We got a client or two but they came through referrals, and no businesses are sustainable using word of mouth. Until I started to create and share content of our industry, things didn't take off. My feed of content would teach me my craft and also provide me with rich material for sharing and creating awareness upon our brand. The subjects that I was reading and sharing the most were Human Resources, inspirational stories, motivation, personal development, career and market trends. I learned that some other subjects such as the rules for applying for Work Permit in Ireland would catch more attention than what people would misjudge as "too much to read." When you curate content for others, you will need to go through the good and bad of content, and most people won't take the time to read about Time Management tricks if they are in the mood for finding a job overseas. Little do they know that finding a job abroad will require them managing their time with excellence so that they can draft a plan and execute. Therefore my content, or the content that I claim the association with our brands, went from quick readings to substantial material that needed to be put in practice.

I also started to write my stuff. I don't have many authored articles published since I am a bigger fan of "short posts." But I wrote about my story; my opinion on the future of jobs and the recruitment industry; a review of events; how to use LinkedIn and how having a managing board made of Women is better. The latter surprisingly brought me a few foes. And I realised how content is powerful for positioning. Besides, having your LinkedIn as you blogging platform plays well when people pop your profile and see the number of articles you published. LinkedIn will keep this number highlighted and subliminally sets you apart from people who only share content from others. It is the recognition of the tool that you are putting your opinion out, that you have a voice, and that you are creating an audience. It is awesome when people revert to you to discuss a point or two about what you wrote, and you think, "Wow! This guy is talking to me, nice!" I wasn't being noticed, and our brands weren't being seen until we started playing with content. Not only clients came to us, but fantastic business opportunities as you will read in the next chapter.

Original Content

No matter how good you will be in finding good content to share, nothing will outperform your original stuff. People crave for new things. We are curious creatures, I must say. It doesn't take much efforts to see that when you post a raw image of you shaking hands with another person. The number of views will go way higher since people stopped scrolling to see who were shaking hands. Viewers will take a few seconds to scan the picture, see if they know the people in the frame, the location to finally decide whether or not they want to like or share the post. The majority will not, but don't be too worried about that because on LinkedIn, what matters is the number of Views and not the Likes and Shares. Do you remember that we spoke about the connection that you want people to make in their brains? You will want to make people associate your persona with your activity, with the people you know, and with the fact that you are every day engaging in a new meeting, with new people, closing businesses. Because that is the impression that the viewers will have when they see your raw image taken on your phone of you shaking hands with another person. They might read the text of your post if you bother to write something, and that will increase your reputation if you tell that what was going on there. It is up to you to build this impression with openness and authenticity.

LinkedIn claims that the count of a View means that a views stuck for at least three seconds on your post. That means that they stopped scrolling to see your post. That means that you grabbed their attention. Awesome. Try doing this with the share of an article from someone else containing a Stick Image. You know. Those post-processed edited images that you can buy online that show no authenticity, no branding at all. They are beautiful, with beautiful people an scenery on them, I will give you that, but they are not yours, and people understand that as they scroll. And that won't make them stop scrolling as much.

On the other hand, try writing some text with no image in it to see the Views up there. You will see how people are judgmental and curious. They want to read your opinion about anything, but they also want to catch your mistake, your misspelling. They will admire you for having the courage to write anything publicly because most people can't just do it. Your raw texts need to be meaningful, though. Don't go there and post about the weather or last night's game because you don't want to look shallow. Avoid themes such as politics and religion too unless they are tied to what you do professionally. People don't care about your opinion on those things, and they might refrain from referring you to an opportunity just because they don't agree with your view.

Your original content can also come in the format of a quote, that could even come fitted with an image or not (See the chapter about the tools to use with LinkedIn.) If it comes from the heart, push it. Even if that has meaning only to you, I am sure that some people will also relate to it. A quote can be a sentence or two surrounding the same subject. In essence, it is a thought that you just had it, but you were too afraid of sharing, until now. Good quotes surround the motivational or inspirational aspect of our lives. Did you wake up at 5 AM to work for the first time? Are you grateful for getting that promotion? Do you feel compelled to share an accomplishment? Share it now. The world needs your thought. Your connections will rank you a person of opinion. Do that often, and your connections will start liking as the Views hit higher. Make a comparison if you can. Place the same text with and without an image. Use the same day of the week, let's say, Wednesday morning. On the first week, post the text you built with a free image taken from Unsplash.com (More on that to come too.) On the second week, post the text without the picture. See how the Views will hit higher and get the same conclusion that I did that people are now programmed to tune off what they interpret as a Stock Image. Get rid of that, therefore. Stick to the Stock Images only when you share things from others, industry-related topics that we will be discussing in the next topic. And when sharing a quote or a meaningful thought that you just had it, make sure that it is yours, and tell the world that you have an opinion.

Curated Content

You will need to mix a good amount of industry-related Shares with your original content. Let's say that this is for advertising your skill sets and disguising your original content (that is for entertaining and awareness of your brand.) Yes, you read that well, your original content will be your Show whereas the Curated Content will be the Advertisement. With

THEY WILL ADMIRE YOU FOR HAVING THE COURAGE TO WRITE ANYTHING PUBLICLY BECAUSE MOST PEOPLE CAN'T JUST DO IT.

the difference that you will do that more often than pushing original content in the beginning. In the ideal scenario, though, you would become a content machine (no reference here to Dan Norris' excellent book.) that creates content on the go, documents every little professional and personal initiative and posts it all online. Well, you might know a few guys online that I am referring to, and you know how these guys are claiming the Social Media to themselves. That is where we all want to get to with the use of LinkedIn. Back on earth, the content shared from others will help you leverage your brand immensely, and the results can be noticed in a matter of weeks. Ideally, you will be sharing content from others three to four times a day, and skipping the Sundays, since no one goes to LinkedIn on God's day apart from Entrepreneurs (who work every single day.) and Marketers split testing something. You will do that outside the work hours, between 8:30 and 9:30 in the mornings, between 12:30 and 13:30 in the afternoons and between 5:30 and 6:30 on evenings. But please use this as a starting point to test your audience. If you don't have an audience, you will create your audience during the times known to be when people are more likely to be scrolling their LinkedIn timelines.

People will consume LinkedIn many times a day. I consume LinkedIn from fifty to one hundred times a day; I know that for a fact. But you will want to get them in the mood or on their work-mode. In the suggested morning slot, they are popping their phones as they sit on their chairs sipping a coffee and small talking with colleagues. Viewers will be more likely to hit the Like button as they feel energised by the Caffeine. In the suggested afternoon slot, they are either leaving or arriving from lunch, their minds are confused and are usually in a hurry. Therefore, they are less intended to subscribe to a page or event you might be sharing. In the suggested evening slot, they feel like they haven't done much on the Social Media on that day and they feel like they are missing a whole world of possibilities, so they like and share the things that are at their reach as they scroll. That makes them feel better, and a new hope is established, and tomorrow they will set that Instagram account and start posting everything. It never happens. But not for you. You are posting now; you are "wild" on LinkedIn and people are starting to notice. You meet a former colleague from another job still connected with you on LinkedIn, and they say: "I saw your post on the other day saying that you applied to that Graphic Design course, how is it going?" And you feel every little cell in your body grateful for the day that you started engaging online and the hope that opportunities will start to come soon. That is the fuel that you were expecting to keep your content machine working.

Industry-related subjects will make your Curated Content as I previously wrote. But what does that mean, exactly? You read, right? If you are reading this book, I will take as an assumption that reading online is your "bread and butter" when it comes to learning. It has never been so easy to consume and share content online. Though we are aiming LinkedIn at this stage, you will love to see that not only can you share content to multiple Social Networks at once but that you can schedule the Shares as well. We will be discussing this in depth later in the book, but I want to flag to you that the times suggested above for you to share content from others is achievable by using free automation tools online. And we will see them later. My aim here now is at creating on you the habit of sharing after reading. Do you know that little Share icon? You got it. Hit that every time you read something online, that relates to your industry. You are in Health and learned about the new transplant methods that Doctors are researching in Israel. You are still in College and know that one day you will become a Doctor, but the post about new findings about the cure of Cancer is the perfect match. It is related. It is not like you are in IT and pushing content about Health. You are in Heath and pushing content about Health that you just read (or partially have done so.) You are a Civil Engineer and read about the housing crisis in Dublin. How the renting prices are incredibly high, and that the Immigrants are paying the bill and all. Is this related to your industry? Hell, Yes! Go there and hit the share button and let people know that you are consuming content and learning on a Saturday evening instead of being in a Pub drinking and complaining about the prices of your rent. And if you have a contrary opinion about the article, it is even better to add some of your comments on the top of the post to advocate for what you believe. It is your voice. Never heard before. Now learning, hungrier than ever for new content to share and for an opportunity to print your name together with your industry to people's minds as they scroll their timelines.

Wise Subjects

We teach people about our programmes to post. More than teaching, we encourage them to make themselves known in their industries by posting what they read and what they do. It is evident to us the growth of people who share and the anonymity of the people who don't. I am yet to define a relationship between how success and the reach of their goals are related to their online activity. I must admit that they have their new profile produced by us on their side. But you too have now what it takes to fix that. Your new profile will bring you the needed confidence to act online. The courage to post the raw photo of your computer as you research for that essay. The confidence to post the thought that you had this morning about going back to school because of an insight you had on yesterday's conference. The courage to post your handshaking with your new partner after lunch with half-burger on a plate as the background. You too can be creative to attract your audience. Most people, the most significant majority, will ignore your posts. But that doesn't mean that they are not creating the association between you, your industry and your activity as they scroll. You will care about the Views too, and realise that when any of your followers hit the Like button, they are displaying your face to their audiences. On LinkedIn, a Like has the same effect as the Share concerning how they are spread from one network to the other. The Share, however, if made on a post coming from a company page on LinkedIn will encapsulate the post, the logo of the company and a button to follow the company. That is how you will increase your company page if you have one.

Opportunistic Content

There is a type of content that is very effective that I see very few people using it. The kind of content that goes associated with another piece of content of another person, not necessarily a person with more connections than you, as either a comment or a post over a Share. On LinkedIn, you must be commenting on people's posts to attract new followers and connections, and consequently, opportunities. When you comment on someone else's post, their connections will see your comment, and everyone who once liked or commented on that posts will also be notified about your comment. People feel the urge to click on these notifications more than you might think. And that is your sweet face and a link to your profile playing again. We will see on another chapter, how you will leverage new connections from visits to your profile, and being visible on people's timelines and notification boards is one of the best ways to attract people to your profile. Attracting people to your profile will increase your followership, increasing your followership will be crucial for the content creation work you are doing in parallel. You are "feeding the beast", excellent approach.

Being connected to people and following what they post is also a great way to spark creativity because they have different goals than you but yet, they have similar strategies. Being posting is the similarity, and as long as they are posting, they are also cultivating and nurturing a network of engaged people who are a given environment for you to play the opportunistic post.

As I write this book, I engage online. Not at the same time, of course. But I split my days to make this happen and yet, I cannot leave plenty of other tasks left alone. I have a few businesses to run, and to me being online is the way that I create awareness upon what we do, and it is how I increase my reputation as a trusted Entrepreneur. I only have to do this once for my

EVERYTHING YOU DO ONLINE SHOWS TO PEOPLE THAT YOU BELONG TO A TINY GROUP OF PROFESSIONALS WHO ARE DOCUMENTING THEIR LIVES.

persona, and all my projects, initiatives, partnerships and businesses benefit from it. That is why the Social Media and LinkedIn are wonderful tools for your growth, no matter what line of business or phase in life you are. But I have a routine to use LinkedIn, and you will see this in the following chapter later in the book. When I am making my sprints during the day, my radar is actively looking for opportunities to engage and take advantage of something. This is how it works, people! Don't give me the criticism now; we are all creating and attracting opportunities, remember?

One of the opportunist practices that I like is the one where I comment on someone else's post describing how my day was. I usually use especially busy days to do this. Days that I had multiple businesses meetings, visits to clients. Days that I magically accommodated a good level of exercise and at the end, I could have quality time with the family. Such days have all the components that you need to sell how special you are and impress people. Not only your people but if you are doing this on another person's post, their people too.

So, let's say that you stumbled upon a post that is a text where a connection you have is describing how their day was. A person who does that is already fishing for opportunities, and they are not concerned if you will comment on their post and tell how your day was. This is actually what they want as not only will that enrich their post but bring their profile visibility on your timeline as well. You are dealing with Pros, Dude. And you will soon become one of them too. Make sure, therefore, that you trade those little aspects of LinkedIn well. On your comment, you have the opportunity to "sell without selling" what you do. If you went on an interview in the morning and met someone in the afternoon to talk about a business initiative. If in between those two meetings you had a call with the local school where you volunteered for a job with sick kids. If after your last meeting you wrote an Email for a company in Norway that might resell those old pieces of equipment you still have from a past business venture. If you got home on time to jog and watch a documentary on the TV that sparked on you your next move.

Everything sells! Everything shows to people that you belong to a tiny group of professionals who are documenting their lives. Don't you want to document your life? Are you still living by the concept that you need your private life? That is gone. The world spins in a different way, and this won't change. Haven't you realised that communication, all communication, will be made through Social Media? That your life will be scrutinised before you get a chance on anything, and the ones practising the self-selling online will be the ones getting the opportunities first? Obscurity is gone. Past gone. And LinkedIn is the ideal place for you to practice your entrance into the new world. A world where ordinary people inspire you. You watch and judge their lives and appreciate the fact that the challenges they face are similar to yours. That the opportunities that they are getting create other opportunities for you. A world where people have access to open ideas and solutions to problems that once were solved by the governments and corporations only. This massive common sense built-in by the Social Networks where information and data are created by people, to people. Have you ever thought that the world needs your story? Evolution needs your story. You are finally set to play a role in this world. And the way you do this is through your content.

Constant Engagement on LinkedIn

The world is made of stories. And I wish I could write my entire story here. I have been blessed by the fact that I can easily track back a story to a point where I can identify how it started. Have you done it? Try it. Any story. If you are married, pick, for example, the story of how you met your partner. Track it back to its origins and remember what specific action that you took led you to meet that person. Not the phone call, or the event that you went and met your partner but what made you make the phone call or go to the event on that day in the first place. Look how that triggered a whole sequence of events that brought you where you are now. No matter how your life is with your partner now (or the lack thereof) you were in control of that first step you took. Now, project this to your current endeavours and to the things that you want in life. Can you reverse engineer the steps that you need to take towards a significant goal? Can you reverse engineer your next step? Yes, just the next step. Break down in small steps and see your major goal unveiling in front of you. Life works this way. I am probably, and hopefully, midway through my life (I am forty-two), and I only realised this recently. I understood that you couldn't control all your actions towards a significant goal, but you are in complete control over your next move. You can't see the world of opportunities that arise once you accomplished your next step. I have my eyes on my primary goal. My "big picture" is still a few years ahead of me. The stories below tell a little bit about my journey as an Entrepreneur and how LinkedIn played a role on all of them. I never planned things to happen this way. I only took the first step to trigger a world of possibilities.

A Marketer from Poland

Part of my content is related to Personal Branding. The term that is used loosely to describe one's online activity. I belong to the group that claim that having online exposure is not the same as being a brand. You become a brand when you satisfy a few conditions that transcend the Internet and the Social Media. It will probably be a subject of another book that I will write as I practice live this workshop about Personal Branding, where I state the nine drivers that make up for your brand: Reason, Communication, Emotion, Presentation, Authenticity, Uniqueness, Consistency, Authoring and Marketing.

As you can see for yourself, these are aspects that can be developed in spite of Social Media. The Internet and the Social Networks are only tools that will help you get there faster and to a broader audience. But don't go there and post a few things and tell people that you are a Personal Brand.

The fact that we discussed these points very often and held events on the subject attracted connections to me. This guy from Poland once messages me saying that for a little while he was following what I was posting and we kept a conversation, liking and sharing each other's posts until he referred me to a famous American Podcast about Sales. It was awesome being interviewed by the guys from Fort Lauderdale and talk live about our initiative of holding free events about Personal Branding and Personal Development in Ireland. Having my experience noticed and the opportunity to expose our endeavours to another Continent improved our reputation and brought us a few new clients. I am now due to pay him back the favour, and I plan on inviting him to be one of the Keynote speakers in one of our upcoming large conferences next year. We are finally set for coffee later this month to shake hands finally.

An Executive from Ireland

Having a business is chasing opportunities. We saw an online call from the European Commission for companies to join the Digital Skills and Jobs Coalition as a member organisation. We described our initiatives towards the lack of talent in Europe and qualified to enter. Chasing further for opportunities to collaborate in the Irish level, where we are based, I found the local coalition, and I was invited to a few steering committee meetings where we discussed practices to attract talent to the country and how to make regulations more flexible. Being together in a boardroom table with members and representatives of the Irish Government has been an incredible experience. I even had the opportunity to meet the Minister of Jobs at the launch ceremony of the local coalition. Because of our online exposure, the content we post that shows our efforts to move people from odd jobs back to their area of expertise; we gained notoriety and recognition. We exhibited at their conference in Brussels and filed a few pledges to help mitigate the lack of talent in Europe. Not bad for a post on the social media they made and that we followed through.

But it wasn't until one of the board members of the local coalition introduce me to the CEO of one of the most prominent Colleges in Ireland as a reference in the field of immigrant labour that I open my mouth to say "What?!" It is incredible how people are creating an opinion about you and that you have no idea about it. LinkedIn has this power when you are actively engaging in it. I imagine the conversation between them that somehow got into the career development that the College needed to apply to students and graduates. How come the Executive thought of me and my business and made the referral? I had no personal relationship with him, never actually spoke directly with him, and he makes the kindest referral that will make our company the College's Learning and Development partner with a few conferences and workshops lined up through the end of 2018 already.

An IT Guy from Germany

Another connection that made us thrive was with an IT guy from Germany who works in Ireland in a Multinational. We don't know each other either, and yet he changed the course of our businesses drastically when he advised me to meet one of his Brazilian friends who has a Software Studio in Dublin. The guy was following our posts and somehow noticed our initiatives to help Startups with a model that is unique in the country: We don't give money, we come up with all the work that is missing to launch the business idea in exchange for equity. A model that is authentic and solves the main issue many Startups have with Administration, Finances, Human Resources, Marketing, etc. The Software Studio was lacking attention and had two beautiful products dedicated to the Language Schools already in the market. They had a few paying clients but nothing else. No administrative tasks, no finance, no strategy and no Marketing. When I met the founder of the company, our empathy was immediate. As a software developer myself, we spoke about past and current trends, he showed me the software, and we scheduled another meeting to talk about what good we could bring to the table. Later on, we set a date for signing the agreement to collaborate, and I met his other partner who is a successful young Brazilian who owns a few Language Schools in Europe. We spoke about business trends this time and made sure to make my inputs about IT Governance, Marketing and Accountancy matters. Signing this agreement was only the start of a collaboration that would bring us plenty of other businesses and our strategic positioning in a new industry. Signing this agreement would also bring us visibility to other businesses and prominent people that generated new partnerships.

If I hadn't followed through the call to meet the founder of the Software Studio, and now my personal friend, I wouldn't have gotten into businesses that complemented our Ecosystem of products. Thanks to that, our main business is now immersed in the EDTech world, building technologies to Education systems and a new product that will revolutionise how kids and Home-Schoolers consume their content and learn. In the personal side, I have been exposed to a whole new set of opportunities, and I am now appointed to lead the commercial team of the top sales exchange students Agency in Brazil: A business that will increase the awareness upon our brands and consolidate our business in the HRTech and EDTech industries in Europe. Incredible how all this was triggered by a guy who saw my posts about Startups.

An Investor from India

What good can an investor do to a business? And what good can a business do to an investor? That is the story of the investor who came to us through LinkedIn after connecting with me declining services that I wasn't offering. When I connect with people on LinkedIn, as you will see in the following chapter, I usually reply with a custom message depending on how I judge the connection will be beneficial to me and my businesses. Sometimes, the title used by the new connection is misleading (nor everyone is caught up by the modern problem-solving Tagline, or they haven't read this book yet) so it happens that my custom message goes oriented by what I read and see on my new connection's profile and activity.

This guy, who shall remain nameless to protect his and my partners, is associated to a big Recruitment Agency and therefore I followed up with my general custom reply that I send to connections that I don't see any immediate benefit. As I evaluate any new connection that I make on the network, I always try to establish what good can come up from that new relationship, and I try to establish a quick prediction of what can happen if I follow through. I also check what connections I have in common with that person, and sometimes this will give me a new insight into my custom and the tailored message that I send after connecting. I also think about what I will give to my new connection. Even before taking or asking anything, I give away something. It can be the date of a new free event we are holding. It can be the recommendation of a new book I just finished reading. I can be the link to a free resource. And, it can be what I like the most, which is congratulating the custom Tagline that the person is using as I love seeing this pattern coming to live from different trends and sources around the LinkedIn world.

On that specific connection, curiously, he came back to me after connecting saying that he already had "someone doing his branding for him." I was caught by surprise because I wasn't offering my services to him as I never do it straight away after a connection. But I guess that my profile spoke louder, and he saw in my profile what I was all about it and assumed that a sales pitch would follow up after we connected. I nevertheless replied politely saying that I was connecting with someone who had looked at my profile (as you will see that this is a great way of increasing your network) and that I wasn't soliciting anything. Silly me to believe that he was the prey in that conversation where I was the one being checked out about my businesses and what I was building. It turned out that this guy from India, despite his "corporative" Tagline, also represented a group of investors from Asia and UK, and that they were searching for new investment opportunities in Ireland, especially in the Education industry. You read above, correct? What other connections led me to be involved in and that my ecosystem was increasing due to new product launches and the possibilities that we followed through.

From that, we went for coffee a few times, and we discussed a few ways to work together. We progressed to see that his group was looking for something bigger to put their money in, and though I wasn't the right fit for them, I wasn't looking to give away control of my companies anyway. But we kept the conversations going on LinkedIn until he referred me to a group of researchers that are now helping us refine one of our HR products. And I could do the good for him too by referring him to one of the owners of the Language Schools that I partnered on the Software Studio I mentioned before. Yes, that one that I came to know because of the IT guy who was seeing my posts on LinkedIn and thought of telling me about the unsupported Founder. Incredible ramification, isn't it? Could I predict this? Definitely not. Can you go more in-depth on any new interaction on LinkedIn so that you can be faced with opportunities? Definitely yes. Something good is likely to happen to you too.

From Where You Belong, Doing What You Do Best

The type of connections you have and the kind of content you create will define these ramifications. LinkedIn has the power of putting things together and it makes those silos of themed information. The more you create content about innovation, and connect with

YOU ARE IN CONTROL OF HOW YOU WANT TO BE SEEN ON LINKEDIN.

people into venturing, the more you will be exposed to the Startup world. The more you connect with the software development industry, the more you will be exposed to new trends, frameworks and that piece of code that you can show to your team on next week's meeting. The more you talk about that medical device that you specialises on, the more curiosity upon your profile you will generate from Doctors and hospital Managers. You are in control, think of that. You are in control of how you want to be seen on LinkedIn. I moved from being a Software Developer to become a Businessman. Though the majority of my working years were with coding, people don't refer to me anymore with programming related subjects. I don't receive .NET or SharePoint job opportunities as I used to get (apart from Recruiters who don't bother to read my profile to see that I ride different waves nowadays.) Therefore you can, and you will give opportunities to these opportunities to happen to you.

LinkedIn is so complex. The possibilities are endless, and the prediction that a conversation is going to lead you somewhere is only a loose guess. I love seeing, though, what comes next. Whether it is the default "thumbs up" that the tool gives as a quick reply, or if the person will also establish a mature conversation that will lead you to something more meaningful, LinkedIn will take you to a different place that you were before starting the conversation. What I wanted with this chapter was to show you real examples of what happened after following through a new connection or communication that looked completely useless at first. New initiatives and partnerships arose from these interactions. Therefore, I am here to tell you to go deep into any communication. You cannot know what ramifications the Universe (of LinkedIn) has planned for you. But you must bet on them. I hope this can cause some effect on you as this is part of your new thought regarding how LinkedIn will attract you the opportunities. Opportunities that you cannot even see because they are out of your reach now. They are obscured by what you can't predict because you are still not taking the next step with the tool. You are still too afraid of being judged and being passive on LinkedIn won't take you far. It will merely keep broadcasting to you the default: Endless job positions from desperate Recruiters in need to meet their sales targets. If you are in business, good luck if you play dead on the tool. I can't count how many conversations, and calls, and Emails, and visits to a local coffee shop I made to trigger these businesses that started on LinkedIn. I take all chances. It is beautiful, yet curious, how a business tool can be in the middle of all this. I can't believe that its Founders haven't thought of that at the beginning: That they felt that the tool would be triggering a world of possibilities to people. But I guess that they kept seeing the results and how people were thriving using the tool that they kept modifying things to enable that. To automate the right content for the people based on their habits and the industries they are involved. To allow customisations to that allows professionals to be creative in the way they interact with people. The bottom line is that business is made of people, whether it is a new job, your first shot or anything more significant you seek, conversations are supposed to be made so that you too can unveil the opportunities. From conversations, you will know that the company you want to work for will open a new branch in Denmark and that French speakers are also a must. From conversations, you will know that the factory you would be perfect for will hire fifty new staff, and the specific requirements they have. From conversations, you will understand that a Bank is granting seed money to fund your new business venture, and how you get under their skin. From conversations, you will know about a person who can be your next right hand in the business or a person who will do the Filmmaking for a lower price. If you are not actively engaging you will keep getting more of the same, you have now, and I assume that if you got this book, you want something more from the tool. Thank you for believing that LinkedIn can take you there because it is taking me where I want to be.

Attracting Opportunities with LinkedIn

You have seen how to create a "killer" LinkedIn profile that is not your Mr Recruiter please-give-me-a-chance that most people use. You have seen that a profile based on your story brings you the possibility to tell the world about your journey and that this establishes a rich environment for your industry-related keywords that will help LinkedIn combine the right content and people that will bring opportunities to you. You have learned that you are in control of that. That you can attract the things that you want, and that you must follow through to make that happen. Thanks for sticking around because, in this chapter, you will see practical examples of how you will engage with people. How to react, how to approach, and how to dig for an opportunity. You will see how company pages, especially the ones that you want to work for, are the perfect environment for you to find decision-makers in your industry. How you can engage with them slowly, build a relationship until it is time for you to ask for a shot directly. You will see how LinkedIn groups are designed, and how you can create the subject matter group that will set you a leader in your space. You will get more confident with the use of automation tools that will help you from grammar to push a bunch of posts through the week. You will see how to configure LinkedIn to work for you, as you sleep, as you take care of other things related to your master plan, and as you follow up with the connections, you kept nurturing. You will see my daily routine on LinkedIn and how I make several engagement sprints during the day. You will see that in detail, and I genuinely believe that this will wrap up things for you in a positive way. I truly think that if you do what I did, or even if you create variations of my process, you will succeed. Well, you took the first step of getting this book. And I hope to engage with you online anytime soon.

Watch Fifty Profiles a Day

The goal here is to make people visit your profile and increase your network, organically. You will hit their profiles first as the first interaction with them. You research and find someone's post in your timeline (where LinkedIn is doing their job to combine posts of your industry, from people in your industry) that has a significant number of Likes and open each of the profiles listed. That will work better if you are using a desktop version of LinkedIn so that you can open the profiles on another tab of the browser. You will need to stick for a few seconds on each profile to make sure that LinkedIn will track your View in the "Who viewed your profile" section of their profiles. You want them to hit you back with another View so that you can ask for the connection and increase your network. It is a great trick that shows people that you have been looking around and don't care about being tracked. LinkedIn is supposed to work this way, though, we can prevent people from seeing that you looked at their profiles, and I won't discuss this topic here for not agreeing with such configuration allowed by LinkedIn. Therefore, leave it open, and get the benefits of exploring new connections that will substantially, and organically, increase your network.

It is not certain, though, that the people that you are listing on someone else's post will be on your industry. They can come from all sorts of sources since you can't control the types of connection that your connection has. That is the reason why you are hitting a good number (fifty) to increase the possibilities. From that number, some will ignore the fact that you hit your profile and they won't hit it back. Some will hit, and you will ask for the connection (with a custom message that we will see soon.) In average, you will make from twenty to thirty per cent of new connections just from that practice. About the people who are not in your industry that might hit your profile back, you will always have the chance to double check if the connection is right for you. I would say to go for it since you want people who collaborate well on the network. These connections were once linking another post, and that somehow means that they are active on LinkedIn, so you want them. I get acquainted every day with people from all over the world with whom I connect in this way. We will see that the custom and tailored message that you will be sending you to grab their interest to your network. And as you will show them that you are taking the care to write personal messages, even if they say that you are "just connecting and increasing your network with amazing people." they are more likely to remember you: especially if you are posting and creating content actively on LinkedIn. We have seen how opportunities can come to you, right?

Doing this exercise as part of your daily routine will bring you disappointment as well. You will notice the high number of Recruiters who configure their LinkedIn to hide their names in your "Who viewed your profile" section. Shame on them! That is just one of the thousand reasons that makes me believe that the Agency Recruiters are not here to stay much longer. In such an open and fair environment as LinkedIn, what type of leverage are they trying with this? To me, that sends a message that they can investigate you but please don't call me back. They are investigating the availability and the skill set of a professional (you) and sending you a message for you that you must not try to connect them back because they don't want to help you only sell you. They are checking their inventory. Thinking about a way to get to your weakness and play with you. That is why I am the biggest advocate that you as a professional must go directly to the companies using the relationship strategy that I am proposing here in this book.

Company Pages

I once told a story to a group of attendees of one of our Workshops. I told them that about a dream that I was seeking a new job, desperate for a new opportunity when I went to an event. The event was in a hotel. Therefore the lobby was full of people from representing multiple companies in a specific industry. They were all discussing how nowadays it is difficult to attract talent to their businesses, and that retaining good people was even more difficult. One of the groups was discussing their internal policies to retain personnel, their extended paid holidays policy where they would pay for the families of their employees to travel along, flight tickets and all. Another group discussed their investment on research that their collaborators had access to capital to test and buy equipment and that was one of their most important programmes to develop new IoT (Internet of Things) technologies to a new world. Another group on the corner of the lobby would discuss their patterns of success in the Biotech industry and their participation in government-funded research to find the cure for the Cancer. A more conservative group had their executives all dressed up, discussing how many associates became junior partners on the past couple of yours, and that they were proud about the retention of their excellent Attorneys, and that would create credibility and positioning in the market.

AGENCY
RECRUITERS ARE
NOT HERE TO STAY
MUCH LONGER.

I told the attendees of our workshops about this dream. And I said to them that I wasn't the only job seeker in the hotel, but everyone would have the chance to stick around with the groups, ask about their projects and initiatives. They would meet people from within their industries and get acquainted. The professionals belonging to the groups would also make questions, and all the time they would bring new subjects for discussion. Always about their specific industry, and always related to the company or brand that they worked. Inside each group, it was easy to identify who was leading the conversations, who was passive, who was making questions and who was taking notes. You could see someone leaving the group momentarily and coming back with a new thing to discuss. You could quickly identify the decision-makers on each group, and who was allowing people to enter the group and talk. Parallel conversations inside each group could also be noticed, and sometimes, a third or fourth person would be called up to answer a question or two.

I told the attendees of our workshop that this place exists and that this place is called LinkedIn. More specifically, the company pages on LinkedIn where people from the same company post, discuss and interact on subjects that are related to the initiatives of their business. A place where you can identify the people who decide, the people who are passive using the tool and the people who are listed but never interact with their network. A place where you can easily list who works nearby you, and who works in a branch in a country that you want so bad to live. A place where you don't depend on Recruiters to give you a chance because you can create a direct relationship with people who can give you a chance. A relationship that is not easy to establish but with patience and strategy, you can (and you will) build rapport and claim your next opportunity, most of the time without even using your boring paper CV. Indeed this place exists, and it is highly underused.

I also make an analogy and paint a picture of you coming to the lobby of one of the companies that you want to work for, any company, any size, with a megaphone dictating your skills, your achievements, how many languages you speak, how friendly and persuasive you are. Of course, if you do that in real life, security will come and get you, therefore don't do it. But I bet that I just made you think about your attitude that needs to change. Your passive attitude is not right, and that is why you are looking for your next opportunity in the wrong way. Relationships come with trust, and relationships bring you opportunities. You are not failing in creating your relationships; you are failing on establishing trust first. And please pay attention to that. The same "pushy" attitude that you have chasing an opportunity you will have after you get the job or the client, that is how they see you.

I deal with many people coming from many

countries looking for a better life for them and their families. I always make sure that I meet in person a professional who buys our programme online because I need to feel from them what they want in life. Of course, I have the most extraordinary people in my team who do the job of assessing their careers and building their strategy for the next years. But it is only when I meet the person that I truly understand who they are. I read their CV's and LinkedIn's, and though they are prepared for excellence, I can never get their true essence from what is written. That is why we also produce their videos as part of our deliveries for them because we want them to explore the fact that the rapport that they need to create with their next employer or client not always can be established with the use of an online tool. Therefore the video fits perfectly into the process of bringing your face-to-face meeting to the online world. It is the missing piece of the puzzle if you think that not only are you doing something that other professionals are not doing it but also your peers will trust you once they watch you on screen. There is even the "celebrity factor" caused on people who believe that they are hiring someone who was featured online and that this would be great for their brands having someone like you around.

Therefore if you are failing to build trust and rapport, you are struggling to attract opportunities, and that is why your history of success is printed inside a few drawers in Human Resources offices. It is a very reduced chance you have with this approach. The paper CV. Besides, people won't read as they used to. Our attention is dedicated to different types of media lately. Therefore you must play with these cards now. You won't change the fact that the paper CV is turning obsolete and that you must resort to new ways of communicating your skill set and history of success in the past. Generating trust, however, has never been easier, wouldn't you agree? That is the silver lining if you believe that if the world is giving you other means to get attention and that the most significant majority of people are still struggling with their small thoughts of spamming their CV's everywhere they can, you are in advantage if you start using alternative ways to attract your next opportunity.

The company pages on LinkedIn are the perfect place for that. You will build a database of companies that you feel like they are a good fit for you. Do that outside LinkedIn. Create a spreadsheet or something and go listing all the names of brands that you would love to belong. If you are in Europe, think about the fact that 95% of the companies are SME's (Small Medium Enterprises) and that almost never you should put all your bets on the big names. The methodology that we propose here might not work very well with the big ones due to their bureaucratic processes and spread decision making. You will want to list the small shops, prominent brands, Startups, NGO's even. Make a good list that is flexible concerning industries, think about the related sectors, vendors of the companies that you listed, the materials they produce, who buys, who competes. Make a mind map, perhaps, and take the first step of your strategy of defining the battlefield. Establishing where you are going to attack first, and ultimately, who is going to hire you or buy the product or service that you sell.

Then you will find these companies on LinkedIn and follow them. You will feel surprised by the fact that there will be companies with a minimal presence on the network. If you are in Digital Marketing, this might be an opportunity as well. The possible absence of their company pages will require from you to search alternative places, Facebook maybe, though the process of finding who decides will be more difficult. Put on your spreadsheet a column with the Url of their online presence and make sure that everyone has a way of being found online. Your next step will depend on that.

On LinkedIn, you will find that you can see how many employees they have. It is a link. Click on it and discover a world of possibilities. Filter by location and find the narrowed number of people who work in your region for the same company that you want to work. These will be your new colleagues. Now they are your prospects, or your sales leads if you will. Do that with every company you listed in your spreadsheet and understand how many people you should be creating a relationship. You won't want to establish an online relationship with all these people, but you can build rapport with large groups of people by interacting with their company pages. On the same page where you listed their names, you can find more useful information about the company's performance, their turnover, their losses. And you can see their online activity, the posts, the announcements, events nearby you. You will stick around for a few moments on each company page and realise what a world of opportunities you could be triggering on these pages. How many people could be connected and contacted? Who decides? Is the CEO of the company active online? Is the Human Resources department posting announcements about an open day? Can you visit their premises, factory? Is there a new product launch, where? You are missing all that, I am afraid.

And if you are up to a more digital approach, you will find that liking, sharing and continually commenting on their posts is highly likely to put your face in front of them, daily, until they start interacting with you. You followed their pages so their content will flood your timeline, it is your playground now. They will talk among themselves, "who the hell is this guy?" They will ignore you at first, but sooner or later, I promise you, you will generate rapport. Do that with all the companies you listed; your chance will increase. Never thought of that, right? I bet that you never thought of going there and making yourself known, with your opinion, mentioning that system

LIKING, SHARING AND CONTINUALLY COMMENTING ON THEIR POSTS IS HIGHLY LIKELY TO PUT YOUR FACE IN FRONT OF THEM, UNTIL THEY START INTERACTING WITH YOU.

you built, the cash you made your past employer save, your awarded research on the university. Believe that you can use all the information you wrote a few days ago on your new profile. Nobody was going to read that there, too many scrolling down. But now you can copy and paste that into a timely conversation on a company page. It will impress people; you will be bold, people will visit your profile after that, you will ask for the connection, in parallel they will see your content creation on their timelines, rapport will increase. Opportunities will be thrown at you because you are starting to be regarded as an authority on your industry.

Companies want two things when hiring: Convenience and the best talent. If you can bring them that, you are all set. Have you ever asked why they resort to Recruitment Agencies? The agencies are capable of turning to them with hundreds of filtered CVs for a specific job position. And they filter and narrow their choices by calling up the candidates and checking for both their eligibility and willingness to take the job. Agency Recruiters know nothing about IT, Health, Marketing or Finance but they bring convenience and what they judge to be the best talent for their clients, the hiring companies. As the Agencies are seen as the only way of getting jobs in Europe for most people, they have fast access to data and information about the candidates, and that is their leverage.

But I am proving you here that there are many other ways to get your next opportunity. A Recruiter calling you is not an opportunity. It is their opportunity since you are their commodity. They are selling your data to your future employer and getting a finder's fee for that. A commission or, in some cases, they will cash upon every single day of your work. And companies are willing to pay for that. Because access to talent is limited for them. But talent is everywhere. And it is your job to put yourself in front of them. Give them the convenience that they are expecting and start making them save on commission paid to Recruiters right there on the spot. Play with it. Play with the fact that you can be at their offices in a half-hour. That you can work for free for a week and let them try you out. That you can prove to them that you can get them a new client a day (if you are in Sales.) That you can fix a mechanical problem that you saw online that they are facing and making them lose hundreds of thousands of Dollars. Show them that you have a strategy for them to bring their product to South America. Be creative, be bold, companies like that. That is the talent on you. Put it out and win in your market, it is your duty.

Tools and Automation
for LinkedIn

Although I kept up with my fourteen to sixteen hours of work a day, I couldn't keep up with the daily writing the way I planned. I wrote more than three-quarters of this book during my holidays with my family as I previously mentioned, but the remainder I had to bring home and finish. And of course, life brought me a whole new set of challenges that affected the progress of the book. The thoughts and my knowledge about LinkedIn had to come naturally in the structure it will be helpful to you, dear reader. No automation tool could help me with that.

But there are automation tools for you to use with LinkedIn. There are means of automating the content that you will push into the platform so that you allow the tool to work for you. While you progress in life, study, work on that project that will give you your raise, or write that business plan that will finally bring that company to growth, LinkedIn can be generating trust about your persona. It is the leverage that you cannot ignore, mainly because you won't be able to keep posting and sharing content in the pace that will make you become the epidemy we spoke about it.

There is a lot of manual processes for you to bring the recommended automation. There are the learnings, the reading, the configurations and the curating of content. You will see that automating your content on LinkedIn and a few other networks will bring you excellent results, but it will be cumbersome to the point that you will argue with yourself whether or not this is worthy of your dedication. Automating your content will be a task that will also benefit your education and your self-learning process. It will be awesome to see how you will force yourself to read more as you educate people. And you will be showing up to people and creating awareness upon your profile as you learn: A cycle that will benefit you immensely.

The fact that you will be learning more will also increase your response time in real life conversations. You will become a source of information so huge that people will stick longer with you in talks. You will always have something to say about almost any subject related to your skill set. This immersion will be so useful to you that you will discover the other side of interactions when you turn the active part on conversations, online and in real life. The time when you were a listener is gone, you will no longer be passive. You will be automating and pushing content and people will interact with you online. You will think that this wasn't happening before. You will feel compelled to communicate. You will keep pushing as you see the results. Online conversations will generate requests for coffee shop conversations, and if you are somehow like me, you will jump on everything. I drop on barely every request for a chat. Well, you read the previous chapter when I describe only a few of my engagements that generated me businesses and opportunities. I have plenty more going on from that. As I write this book, I think of my agenda, and how this has been populated with chats and phone calls that came from LinkedIn interactions, that came from my posting habits, that came from my automation process, that came from my reading and curating methodology that I now unveil to you. It is an essential part of the process. You can have a killer LinkedIn profile but if you don't engage this won't take you far. And even if you participate, if you don't automate part of your process, the engagement will fade out in a matter of weeks. So let's start by pushing one month of content on them, hard and frequent. Let's send a message that you came to stay and set yourself apart from the competition.

Feedly

I used a lot of "Readers" and "aggregators" in the past. I remember that tool from Google that I used to combine the content that I liked, the sources of information in my industry, all the tech-related content that would keep my knowledge current. I then used a tool called "Delicious" that bookmarked the sites and articles that I liked. I also loved and used a lot RSS feeds the sites provided so that you could consume their content on some of these platforms without having to go to each source of information to learn. Every click you saved in a dial-up connection (Millenials, Google it), would be useful.

The speed of the Internet connections increased,

and so did the way we consume content. Reduced Clicks and Scrolls are still essential aspects that will make a piece of content be visited or not. Be shared or not. I haven't visited Google Reader and Delicious for a long time now, and I don't even know if they are still there yet. I haven't used RSS feeds either, but that doesn't mean that I am don't have my sources of content organised.

I use a tool called Feedly that essentially, does the same thing as the ones I used to use: It aggregates to content for me. But like any other favourite and highly used tool on the Internet nowadays, it is fast, easy and intuitive to use. It is on my mobile and my laptop, it is on the Cloud, and it is synchronised. And it is designed for reading and sharing. It has options for grouping your content feeds; it brings you current content, you can bookmark your sources, highlight text within content and mark to read later. It consolidates content by sources, and it shows you in a lovely way "what's new" from the origins of content you claimed as yours. You will search and combine content by themes. The themes that you defined as related to your industry and skill set. A minimum of three to begin with, and don't go over ten or twelve subjects or else you might risk being too broad in your selection of content and confuse your audience.

If you are a Software Developer, you can search for "programming" for instance, and find blogs and publications that talk about this subject matter. If you are in Health, you will want to search this term but also more specific things from your background such as "Neuroscience." If you are in Marketing, you will find plenty to chose. You will find that some sources will bring you as much as three hundred publications a week whereas some will be so complex and rare that will bring you as few as two publications a week. On Feedly, you can "follow" these sources of content. You will follow them based on the quality and quantity of content. You want the quality, of course, you want to find that source of content that no one else is pushing in your region and reach, but you will also wish to find favourite sources that will bring you plenty to read and push into your content queue. Remember, even if you push just a few intelligent posts a week, that won't make you the Epidemy, and that won't help you grow your audience from that. Unless you already built a reputation and an impressive number of organic followers, quantity will be more important than quality in the beginning. Though you will also want to verify the quality of each source you define. And Feedly is the right tool to help you with that.

You will use an aggregator for the mere fact that you want to ease the process of searching, reading and sharing. The more you have in your way; the more significant are the chances that you will get distracted and give up on curating the content that will take you there. You are avoiding the Devils inside you by facilitating and creating a routine that will require just a few clicks. So go online when you finish this book and open a free account on Feedly. The free account won't give you as much as the paid one, but it will be enough for you to start. The free account won't give you the excellent integration with a tool called "Buffer" that we will be talking about shortly in the next topic, and that will require from you an extra click every time you automate the sharing of a post. But it is more than enough to start, and even when you decide to invest in a subscription, their yearly price is quite affordable for most of us.

After creating your account, start by finding the sources that you want to consume. Don't think about posting or sharing now. Don't think about LinkedIn now. Think only about what are the themes that you want to keep learning. In addition to your skill set and background. It won't be about learning things from a different industry but about learning and improving your knowledge about the things that you already know and work around. When you search the terms, you will see that the tool will give you several sources such as Blogs, online Paper publications, technical and corporative Websites. Feedly will show the average number of posts they do, how many followers they have, and you will want to go more in-depth on a candidate to become your source to check the quality of the source. You will find popular Websites that are full of timely articles. Those publications that invest in paid authors to increase their followership and sell

Ads. You will want to follow them too because of the volume and the quality of their text. But you will also want to dig into B-sides publications that will feed you content that no one else has.

At this stage, we are not talking about writing your stuff. If you will be seeking content that is current, smart and frequent, adding the authoring into the mix would put a halt into the process of attacking LinkedIn. Producing your content would be the must but what is the point of writing weekly Blogs if you don't have followership and an audience to read that? You will want to become known to a few people first who interact with your content before you can start introducing your original pieces of content. But you will also want to become an Epidemy and eliminate followers as you gain new ones to create your funnel of opportunities.

Once you have selected and followed a few sources on Feedly, you will notice that you can group these sources by their subject matters. You can give any name to these groupings, and in my case, I put the name of the Company that I am producing content. Yes, we are paid for doing that for other clients who believe in this methodology. Unless they are into something that I don't have the guts to learn, I read their content, follow and automate their content by curating what I believe their audience will like it. We keep the interest of their audience on their products and their funnels working to bring them the clients. I use a

THE MORE YOU HAVE IN YOUR WAY; THE CHANCES ARE THAT YOU WILL GET DISTRACTED AND GIVE UP ON CURATING THE CONTENT THAT WILL MAKE YOU SUCCEED.

single subscription of Feedly we have to combine the content of various themes for each specific client. In your case, you will name these groups with the same term you used for searching in the beginning. If you searched for "Artificial Intelligence" and followed a few publications in this subject matter, go there and group them as such. You will see that the tool created those headings that you make your life easier when you are in the mood of reading only about that specific theme.

And as you read, you will share it. You won't share all the posts straight away because you will need to consider the right time to push the content. Let's retake the Sunday evening. Perhaps another one since you used another Sunday evening for producing you nice and shiny new profile on LinkedIn. Sharing all the posts in the same moment will flood your audience's timelines, and they will be more likely to unfollow you. Though you want to become an "Epidemy", you will start slowly and with the strategy of posting on the same hours and pre-defined days of the week. LinkedIn is a ghost town on Sundays, as I suggested before, and you don't want to waste that excellent Blog post about the future of Bitcoins you just read. You will want to push that on either Wednesdays or Thursdays mornings when you know that people will be more likely to scroll over it, perhaps stop by and read and like it.

You will see that finding the right source, the

themes that resonate with people is an exercise. You must keep up with the work and be ready to evaluate the results and make changes if needed. You will notice that as you post, the viewership of your posts will increase from week one to week two. Likes, Shares and the opportunities will follow. It is magical who this works. And now you have one of the right tools for that: Feedly.

I am definitely at risk to be writing about a tool or a mechanism within a tool that might be obsolete when you get my book. Even LinkedIn might be obsolete when you get this book. But I don't bet on it. And shouldn't you either. Not only should you bet that LinkedIn will be there, but you should also bet that content will create your Kingdom. These tools are here to help you with that. As you use them, you will see how they are designed to attend this specific need. From Feedly, you can share on multiple sources, as I said, but one specific source will allow you to share with other various sources at the same time. The name of this tool is "Buffer", and we will discuss that right now.

Buffer

I read this book called "Content Machine" from Dan Norris once. I don't remember correctly if the Buffer tool was mentioned in there. Probably not. But I remember that the author would go through detailing all these other tools that help you increase your notoriety on the Social Media. What his book has in common with this one is the concept that content needs to be frequent.

You can't keep up with the frequency needed to set yourself apart if you depend on content. You just can't. I can't. And that is why I automate everything. I have set the times for my posts on LinkedIn, Facebook, Instagram and Twitter for all my personal and company pages. I automate post to groups, and I automate posts for my clients. I automate so that I can keep up with the job of reading, curating and scheduling the Shares once or maybe twice a week. It fits in my life. And like everything in life, you will be required to have discipline on it. Make that part of your job of finding a job. Make that part of your job to sell your products. Make that part of your job of finding new clients for your Coaching practice. Make that part of your job of finding members for your local community or movement. You will see that it will be easier to configure your "voice" to the masses and reap the rewards of doing that.

Before I dig into the Buffer thing, I must tell you that I also push loads of real-time content. Thoughts that I just had, a picture that I just took and videos that I force someone to make with me, especially after meeting someone with whom I spoke about their needs or the services that we already provide them (the Opportunistic Content we talked about it.) I get people by their arms, inadvertently, and hit "record." Without thinking on a script on what to say, I use the heat of the moment, and I look at the camera. I always publish the first take, rarely with editing or cuts. I keep small mistakes, redundancies, and words that wouldn't be pertinent if we were filming on a Studio, produced. It is for a different purpose. It is for the Social Media. It is for social selling, for the credibility, for showing people what you are. To show people that you are busy, that you have prospects and opportunities: that you have a life. Some types of content you cannot automate. It loses authenticity and momentum. Sometimes it needs to be "now or never."

I believe in a proportion of three-quarters of content being automated and coming from other sources that your trust, that you read it and carefully selected for your audience. The other quarter is left for your live and timely creations, your advertisements in disguise and your professional life documented. And that is when Buffer will come handy. When you create your schedule you will see your posts on the agenda; graphically you can identify gaps in the content and the days that you are pushing too much. You can view weekly campaigns that will run on every day of the week at the same time. You can easily re-schedule the campaigns once again to another time by using their "re-buffer" button on the posts. And yes! You will have campaigns. You will have the ability to overseeing how many posts you have for a determined theme, when they run and how often. Considering the proportion I suggested, you will see how many posts are customised and how many as Shares from other authors. You will leave it running for a month or two, depending on the type of subscription you have with them.

Like the Feedly tool, Buffer is also free. And they will allow you to connect to three of your Social Media accounts as soon as you create your account. The free account will allow you to schedule the posts only. It is enough for you to start, don't overthink for now. Stick to the routine of planning your ten posts first, and Buffer will tell you when they get your queue emptied. But you must, however, be on top of that by monitoring and checking your queued posts frequently. Well, you will read more often too and get checking your feed of content as well. As I said, you will have campaigns and your editorial calendar, you will kind of become your Marketer, selling the product "You." How nice is that?

The free account will let you feel how beautiful it is to have your Shares working on their own and at the same time for the three networks; you will pick. With time, you will figure that you want to pre-define the time slots that suit you best and Buffer will give you that too. Per the network, you can create slots of time that will build your queue. So let's say that you want to post twice a day for the three networks you picked. Twitter, Facebook and you guessed, LinkedIn. When you have your three accounts connected to your free subscription of Buffer, the tool will give you a dashboard where you can fix the time slots. You can define a time slot on Mondays that are different from the ones on Tuesdays and so on. But for the sake of your new editorial calendar, let's keep it simple and define the same time slots for all the workdays. Remember, the workdays and time slots of your audience, not yours. If you want to amplify your chances of reaching people in California, you will set your Buffer to work on their timezone and then set the time slots to receive your posts. If you want to work somewhere along the beautiful Brazilian coastline, check for the timezones that people are more likely to see your content. And if you want to work in Dubai, you might consider that the Folks over there have their workdays starting on Sundays. Buffer will allow you such flexibility in defining all this, and you will feel at home, trust me.

You will first stick to two timeslots per day, and five workdays as your free accounts won't allow you to schedule more than ten posts in a row. But that won't be a hassle for you. Go there and define 8:30, 12:30 and 17:30, from Monday to Friday and you will see that the table is filled with the times you defined. Though Buffer won't give you the fantastic "Calendar view" they have that would show you the boxes representing posts that you can drag around, with the free account you will see a timeline (or queue, if you will) that will pretty much help you understand what you have planned.

You will grab an Url from your new Feedly page or from an article that you might have in your browser. You will copy the thing and paste on the dialogue box on Buffer that resembles a posting dialogue of LinkedIn and Facebook. You will see that Buffer has all those functionalities of attaching the image associated with the article and bringing the headline of the content. As you configure your first post, you will notice that you can select on the dialogue the social networks that you want to push your content. You will want to make a dent on Facebook and Twitter too for the sake of your debut. Once you have the post fetched you might want to write something that will make you look smart, a comment or a recommendation of why your audience should read the article you are sharing. With everything set, go there and select to either queue your post or schedule to a defined time slot. And that is what will make you love the tool. If you push to your queue, the tool will fit your Share in the next available slot it finds. Share the second post, and the tool will fit it after and so on and so forth. Until it fills the ten slots, you have with your free account.

With your sharing dialogue still open, you might want to opt for scheduling the post instead of filling up your time slots. You might want to define a specific time (e.g. 10:34) for your post to be released. It is nice when you want to publish a post on the exact time that you will be, let's say, in a sales meeting and you want to tell your clients (perhaps even the attendees of the meeting) that you are everywhere. I like using this for campaigns over campaigns that we make. Let's say that we are hosting an event in two weeks time. When we set an event up online, not only does the event go to our mail lists but a whole bunch of posts related to the event are scheduled on Buffer so that we don't become a "slave" of the event. Publishing an event is much more than just enabling its tickets online. You will need to create awareness, anticipation, confirmation and after the event, remarkability. So let's say that we have all scheduled beautifully but as you go approaching the date of the event, there are questions from the people who booked the event, a change or two in the content that you are publishing pieces of it to generate trust or a fantastic thought that you just had about the venue. You will want to set a few things up that were not planned. So the tool will turn handy again when you set those three extra posts for the day before the event. With ten minutes of difference from each other, you will set your comments to go live when people are most likely to be visiting their LinkedIn profile. Sipping coffee when they sit to work at 8:30, when they are restless before they leave for lunch at 12:30 or excited to go home about 17:30.

As you go planning your editorial calendar on

Buffer, you will keep tracking the results of your posts, especially on LinkedIn. The number of Views, Likes and Shares that you had and how people are reacting to your new online exposure. You will understand people and their online habits, and that will make you believe that you will need to adjust your time slots, the frequency and even the type of content that you are pushing. That is all fine. If you are re-evaluating the way you behave online, that is more than excellent. It means that you are up for it, It means that you are progressing towards your opportunities. It means that you believe in the process and the fact that you are using tools to automate your exposure shows maturity. These tools are not designed for Marketers only, they are intuitive, and they are part of a trend that indicates how the next Social Media years will be. What comes next? You might want to ask Gary Vaynerchuck about it; he is the specialist in Social. I have my predictions, and they are pretty much all over this book. What I know is that you have leverage now. You have three things that you did not have before: Feedly, Buffer and the will to make your LinkedIn work for you. The new routine you will establish will guide you to your goals. I am a true believer that Social Media is not optional anymore. It is not something that you can ignore and believe that the opportunities will still come. As I put in the book, it is how the majority of communication will be made, how work will be done and how people will interact. If you are not out there with a voice, who are you? And if you have the ability now to push your voice more often, consistently and annoyingly, who is to say that you can't? The Recruiters? Because I do it and only good things came from this approach. I want this for you too. Please try it. Don't ignore the fact that if you try to create a presence online manually, you won't keep up with the needed pace. You need to automate.

Grammarly

English is not my primary language. Well, I like the way I write, I believe that I have an excellent vocabulary and that I can put my thoughts on paper using a language that ten years ago had its presence in my life only in music and TV shows. Writing a book in English probably crossed my mind when I was living in Brazil, but that looked like an impossible goal. But the world spins, and life takes you to incredible and unpredictable places. And then you learn. You learn that no matter where you go in the globe, human beings are the same, they want the same things, and though they react differently to life aspects, no people are superior. And the English language turned to me as ordinary.

Think about now about how many of my mistakes you found in this book. How many times I went on writing on the past tense, and then came back to recommend something using the present or future tense. Yes, that is me being authentic. You can almost feel the way I talk with people and to the audience of our events. If you know me, you can practically hear my voice tone as you notice some of my grammar mistakes or a lack of structure here and there. I respectfully don't care. I don't care because at the moment that I forgot about perfection and making everyone happy, I was able to put my thoughts in this book.

And it is funny how you relate better to people when you are natural and original. That is why you too must be writing on LinkedIn. That is why you must be using its fantastic blogging platform embedded in the tool as LinkedIn will keep organised your authored content right there together with your profile. When people hit your profile, they will be able to see how many articles you have written, and even though most people won't be in the mood to give an extra click to read them, it plays well when they see that you took the time to write and publish something on your own. It also sets you apart from the competition.

A professional editor will not revise this book. It will not be proofread by a professional. I am writing in the most straightforward editor, and I will paste all the text into Grammarly. Also, my wife will read and fix my "you's" and "your's." Mistypings that Grammarly might not be able to catch. You must trust the tool to revise your authored posts and content as you go. Grammarly will be your best ally connected to your browser or preferred editor to put your commas and conjugations in the right place. Grammarly will tell you when you are using the same word too much and suggest you replace the repetitive word by a synonym. You will learn as you turn smarter to your audience. Your credibility and trust are also there, and that is why I listed Grammarly as a "must have" tool for your LinkedIn presence and strategy.

Unsplash

One of the Websites where I buy templates from once recommended me a place where I could get hundreds of thousands of royalty free images to my content. A place that you could find beautiful images that almost transcends the boundary between original and stock pictures. I kept coming back to this Website for much more than sourcing images to my posts. To be honest, I don't use images that are not mine in my original content, and since Shares from other sources already come with an image, the Unsplash Website turned to be useful for the content of our presentations, and their pictures illustrate the backdrop of our PowerPoint slides. Incidentally, they are part of our editorial calendar for LinkedIn and other networks.

I once went to an event about Startups, and this presenter had a set of slides that caught my attention. Much more than boring bullet points on the screen he would use only images that would remind him about his next topic of discussion. I felt amazed about how simple yet entertaining his presentation was, and that sparked my ideas to create a combination of written content and rich imagery to the presentations we give to our audiences. During the process of rebranding our PowerPoint files, no other Website crossed my mind as I had what I needed with Unsplash. You search, find and download pictures in two clicks and they are always in high resolution. A gift from fellow photographers all over the world who dedicate their time shooting and post-processing stunning images for the masses. Is this an alternative to your regular stock image Website? Yes, surely. Why paying to have pictures that are not exclusive if you can have equally beautiful images for free.

But there is one caveat here. On LinkedIn, you will notice that posts with images will not perform well. People are now programmed to ignore posts that look like published articles, especially if they are not in the mood to read anything. You will notice that content without an image will perform way better than when illustrated. You don't want that to your content so how should you be finding a combination between artwork and content that will grab the attention of your audience?

We discussed how storytelling is useful to create awareness upon your profile. Text-only content will make people stop scrolling as they get curious about your writing. We debated that continually sharing things from others will create a relationship between your profile and a specific industry. As you keep displaying to people what you read and learn, people increase their respect about you, and that means credibility. These two practices must be combined so that you can create an interesting timeline of content and attract opportunities. But what if you could be building the third stream of fresh and quick content that could be as engaging as the text content and as trustworthy as the content you share from others? Combining Unsplash with the fifth tool in this catalogue will bring you that. A tool that will be on your mobile and that will give you a way to write short text over images. A tool that will allow you to use the rich database of pictures from Unsplash and the original text of your articles and thoughts that cross your mind all the time.

The name of our fifth recommended tool is Canva. Not that the free tool does not deserve a topic on its own, but I wanted to have this as extended use of your images. Images that will also come from your mobile phone as Canva can take photos directly on its editor. What is unique about this tool is how easy it is to create fancy and engaging designs within the formats of the most known networks so that you don't have to be worried about the right layout for LinkedIn or Facebook. It is all there. Open an image and fit a text that combined with the artwork sends a message. Try yourself and see how easy it is to write your thoughts as you interpret the image you are using. This is how the Internet get flooded with quotes from all sources, and quotes that motivate people to take action or create an opinion. Quotes that will be coming from you quickly because you won't need to figure out the tool or resource to use. They are all there at the reach of your fingertips. Integrated with your LinkedIn as you hit the Share button.

If you are connected with me, you will stop wondering how I can keep up with the common sharing. Now that you know all the tools that I use to keep producing fast and timely content on LinkedIn creating the Epidemy we spoke about is now your responsibility. It is your responsibility to put your thoughts out together with your planned queue of posts from others that will allow you to be everywhere when people open their timelines. As we previously discussed, your populated line of content will make people stop following you, but it will also attract new people of your industry, people who like the same things as you. Your online activity, especially on LinkedIn, will help you tweak your aim at the right sources and targets. And that is how the opportunities come. I need you to trust in the process. I need you to believe that all this organisation and the configuration of tools are paramount steps that must be taken before you can see the results of the method I propose here. Abraham Lincoln used to say that if he had six hours to chop down a tree, he would spend four hours sharpening his axe. That is what I am proposing you.

Acknowledgements

To every crazy thing that I think about that I have my wife Thalita on board; 22 years together and counting. To my little Instagrammer and YouTuber Anabella. To my Father and Brothers back in Brazil. To my in-laws for their Bohemian lifestyle.

To the Influencers with us on our mission to mitigate the lack of professionals in Europe. To the immigrants all over the world who dared to move for a better and honest life. To the people who are not afraid to work sixteen hours a day, seven days a week.

To the miracles of electronics. To the Outliers. To the Prophets on Social Media. To Medicine, Astrophysics and Engineering. To everyone who was told not to do it and did it anyway. To the challenges we have that don't look so bad when we face them.

Here's my first book ever. I hope you like it.

@felipelodi

About WorkFlow ICT

We enable the career and business of international professionals in Europe by empowering their personal and entrepreneurial Brands.

Since 2011, our team of influencers developed the personal branding, LinkedIn visibility, interviewing skills, body language, presentation, written and spoken English, leadership, time management and the entrepreneurial mindset of professionals, and at a ratio of 73%, they improved their soft and social skills and moved from odd jobs back to their area of expertise.

As an active member of the Digital Skills and Jobs Coalition of the European Commission, we acquired a few other businesses recently and independently launched an ecosystem of HRTech and EDTech products and brands that helped us expand to the UK and Benelux Region.

Know more at:

workflowict.com
meetyourinfluencers.com
idolstudios.com
comeduc.com
vlgio.com

FELIPE LODI

FIRST EDITION

45277759R00128

Printed in Poland
by Amazon Fulfillment
Poland Sp. z o.o., Wrocław